UNDERSTANDING
CRIMINAL LAW

C.M.V. Clarkson is Visiting Senior Fellow at the National University of Singapore.

J.A.G. Griffith is Emeritus Professor of Public Law in the University of London.

Understanding Law
Editor: J.A.G. Griffith

C.M.V. Clarkson

UNDERSTANDING
CRIMINAL LAW

Fontana Press

First published in 1987 by Fontana Paperbacks
Second impression February 1989

Fontana Press is an imprint of
Fontana Paperbacks, part of
the Collins Publishing Group,
8 Grafton Street, London W1X 3LA

Set in 10 point Times

Printed and bound in Great Britain by
William Collins Sons & Co. Ltd, Glasgow

To my students –
past, present and future

Contents

Editor's Preface

This series is directed primarily at two groups of readers: the general reader who wishes to understand what it is that lawyers are talking about and the law student who is told that he is about to study a subject called tort, or contract, or criminal law, or property, or trusts and equity, or public law. These titles convey little that is clear about the nature of their subjects and the extralegal meanings that attach to some – such as contract or criminal law – may be misleading.

Each book in this series seeks to explain what the subject is about, what are the special kinds of problems it seeks to solve, and why it has developed as it has. The books are not at all meant to be summaries of their subjects, each of which covers a complicated area of human activity.

The law student will, in his or her course, be expected to read much longer and fuller texts on the subjects, to attend lectures and tutorials. The books in this series seek to provide introductions to be read early in the course or before it begins. It is hoped that these introductions will enable the student to grasp the essentials before coming to grips with the details. So also, the general reader who wishes to pursue the subject more fully will have to read the more detailed texts.

Although these books are intended to be introductions, they are not meant to be simplifications. These are not 'easy' books, however clearly they are written. Understanding law is not an easy matter. This is not, as is often said, primarily because lawyers use words with special meanings. It is because law has to deal with the complications, both personal and commercial, that people become involved in. We are all as busy as ants, more purposeful and sometimes less efficient. Law tries to regularise these complications and so cannot avoid being itself complicated.

11

The intention of the series will be achieved if the books give the reader a broad perspective and a general understanding of the legal principles on which these different subjects are based.

John Griffith
April 1987

1

Introduction

This book is primarily concerned with the substantive criminal law. Its main focus is on the general principles of criminal liability and the structure of the various criminal offences. Such a study can be meaningful only if one knows what is the purpose of the criminal law and if one examines its rules in that context. This functional approach makes it possible to understand the rationale of the various offences and their relationship to each other; one is in a position to evaluate and criticise the substantive law and, if necessary, to suggest reforms.

Accordingly, this book starts with an introduction to the nature and development of the criminal law, including a brief mention of the purposes of punishment. The second and major section examines the main elements in the construction of criminal liability and the leading criminal offences. The emphasis throughout this section is on the purpose of the criminal law and the rationale of its various rules. In this way the relationship between the various concepts and offences can be stressed, enabling an embryonic theory of criminal liability to emerge. Finally, armed with this understanding of the substantive law, the final section is devoted to a more detailed exploration of the theme running through the whole book, namely, the function of the criminal law.

A. THE NATURE AND DEVELOPMENT OF CRIMINAL LAW

The criminal law is a body of rules listing the various criminal offences, identifying the ingredients thereof (including common elements such as general defences) and specifying the potential

13

punishment. For instance, the criminal law tells us that, amongst others, rape and theft are crimes; it tells us exactly what the elements of these offences are and what potential punishments they carry.

The list of crimes (in the sense of wrongdoing punished by the community) in early law was extremely short, and included as major offences withcraft and incest (Diamond, 1950). For offences such as homicide, wounding, rape, theft etc. the only remedy in primitive law was self-help. As society developed, self-help was replaced by a system of enforced payment of compensation. The harmed victim, or his kin, was entitled to compensation from the wrongdoer. Such offences were thus not perceived as public wrongs affecting society as a whole. Only the victim or his kindred had sustained a loss and was entitled to have this loss made good.

The community at large did however have some interest in such forms of wrongdoing. Even in Anglo-Saxon times severe punishments were meted out against offenders who were unwilling or unable to compensate. By the end of the twelfth century it had been realised that such wrongdoing had implications beyond the simple harm sustained by the victim. First the wider community and then the king began to assume responsibility for criminal justice. Those who had broken the 'king's peace' were brought before the king's judges who were itinerant justices. The charges were laid on behalf of the community by a 'grand jury'. Punishments were imposed that did not involve compensation to the victim. In short, the criminal law began to assume one of its most distinctive features, namely, that it is concerned with public wrongs.

A crime is a public wrong in the sense that the public at large is affected by it. The community is threatened or offended by the crime. For example, the crime of rape does more than harm the victim. Society is threatened and made less secure by the rape: the rapist could strike again. Accordingly, society is not prepared to leave the matter to the victim to seek compensation. Rape is made a crime and society attempts to apprehend the rapist and secure his punishment.

Two related features dominated the early criminal law. First, most offences were extremely broad, covering a wide range of wrongdoing. For instance, there was only one homicide offence, the present distinction between murder and manslaughter coming into existence only in the fifteenth century. Secondly, until the end of the twelfth century it appears that the criminal law was primarily interested in the amount of harm done. Man was punished not because he was blameworthy but because he was an instrument of harm. Such thinking led some primitive laws to punish all instruments of harm. Thus animals could be executed and axes burned. They, and the man who used them, were tainted with evil. Such thinking is still with us today to a certain extent. For instance, if a carving knife were used in a murder we would all regard as distinctly odd (to put it mildly) the man who knowingly used that knife to carve his Sunday roast!

Naturally, this emphasis on the results of action as opposed to the blame attached to the offender was an important reason for the breadth of criminal offences. If a victim was killed, his death alone was critical in defining the offence and so it is not surprising that there was only one broad homicide offence. (Even accidental or justifiable killings such as those in self-defence were embraced within the offence; in such cases, however, a pardon would often be granted by the king, exercising his royal prerogative of mercy.) The present distinction between murder and manslaughter is based very largely on the different degrees of blame attached to the defendant and could hardly have existed in a system of law that did not draw such distinctions.

Towards the end of the twelfth century an important shift in emphasis began to occur and man came to be regarded as a moral agent who could be held responsible for his actions. This changed attitude was probably due to a combination of two strong forces: the growing importance of canon law with its emphasis on moral guilt, and the revived Roman law with its stress on the psychical element of blame in criminal liability (Sayre, 1932). It became important to judge the *quality* of man's actions in the sense of exploring his motivations and the circumstances surrounding his actions. Man, being a responsible moral agent, could be judged in terms of praise and blame in a way in which one would not judge an animal or an axe. A proper judgment of his moral guilt necessitated an exploration of his state of mind. Emphasis began to be placed on the mental element in crime. The concept of *mens rea* (guilty mind) began to develop in English criminal law. (For a fuller discussion of the concepts of responsibility and *mens rea*, see pages 56–8.)

Of course, once the concept of blame was established in the law it was inevitable that sooner or later the broad offences would be subdivided so as to reflect the different degrees of blame involved. Thus when, at the end of the fifteenth century, homicide was divided into two main categories, the division soon came to be based primarily on the presence or absence of 'malice aforethought' – an indicator of a special degree of blame. Such thinking has continued to dominate and inform the structure of criminal offences up to the present time. One of the tasks of this book is to assess whether such an approach is still justifiable and what weight should be attached today to these twin concepts, harm and blame – and, of course, to examine their precise meanings.

Another important, albeit self-evident, feature of the criminal law is that crimes are followed by criminal proceedings. Criminal offences were originally divided into felonies and misdemeanours which was broadly a distinction between serious and lesser offences. This distinction was abolished by section 1 of the Criminal Law Act 1967. Today two sets of distinctions are drawn. First, there is a distinction between serious arrestable, arrestable and non-arrestable offences (Police and Criminal Evidence Act 1984). This distinction refers to the powers given to the police to arrest offenders without a warrant (and other matters affecting police powers). Secondly, crimes are also classified as being summary offences, indictable offences or offences triable either way (Criminal Law Act 1977). A summary offence is one that must be tried by a magistrates' court; there is no jury in such courts. An indictable offence is one that must be tried in the Crown Court where the trial is by jury. An offence triable either way is one that allows magistrates to try the case if they feel that is appropriate and if the defendant agrees.

Apart from the different courts involved, criminal proceedings differ in several respects from civil proceedings. While any citizen can bring a criminal prosecution, it is normally handled by the police and by the Crown Prosecution Service. Generally there is no time limit for criminal proceedings. And finally, the procedure, rules of evidence and rights of appeal are very different from civil proceedings.

B. PUNISHMENT AND SENTENCING

The real distinctive hallmark of the criminal law, however, is that convicted offenders become liable to *stigmatic punishment*. Damages in civil actions, particularly exemplary damages, can seem similar to punishment. Their purpose, however, is to compensate a person for his loss. The purposes of criminal punishment, on the other hand, are more varied and controversial. While this issue will be canvassed at greater length in the final section, it is important at this stage to list the four most commonly stated purposes of punishment. These are retribution, deterrence, incapacitation and rehabilitation. Whichever of these purposes is invoked, the purpose is a public one (as opposed to a private, compensatory purpose). It is the state that is exacting retribution or incapacitating a dangerous criminal and so on. In aiming at its purpose the state is publicly condemning the defendant's actions. This results in a special stigma not attaching to defendants in civil actions – hence the phrase 'stigmatic punishment'.

In the early development of the criminal law punishments were crude, draconian and indiscriminate (in the sense that a wide variety of crimes all carried the same potential penalty). Punishments varied greatly over the centuries: for instance, before 1285 the punishment for rape was castration and blinding. However, generalising somewhat, the punishment for misdemeanours was in the discretion of the itinerant justices, fines and whippings being the most common punishment; felonies were generally punishable by death so that a wide array of offences such as murder, rape and theft all carried the same penalty.

The position today is completely reversed, in that a wide variety of punishments is now available. When dealing with adults, the sentencing judge has the following different types of sentence at his disposal:

(i)   imprisonment (this is usually a 'determinate' sentence, that is, for a fixed number of years, or, for murder and in some other extreme circumstances, an 'indeterminate' sentence of life imprisonment);

(ii)   partly suspended sentence (the offender goes to prison for a portion of his sentence; the remainder is suspended, that is, it only becomes activated if he commits a further offence within a specified period of time);

(iii)   suspended sentence supervision order (the whole of the sentence is suspended and the offender is placed under the supervision of a 'supervising officer' [a probation officer] for a specified period);

(iv)   suspended sentence (the whole of the sentence of imprisonment is suspended and no supervision order is made);

(v)   community service order (the offender is made to perform unpaid work such as gardening, decorating or repairing the homes of the elderly or the handicapped for a specified length of time, between 40 and 240 hours);

(vi)   probation order (the offender is placed under the supervision of a probation officer for a specified period of between six months and three years; the order may include various requirements such as that the offender reside at a specified place – usually an 'approved probation hostel', or that he attend a specified 'day centre' [for not more than sixty days], or that he submit to treatment for a mental condition, and so on);

(vii) deportation order (of a foreigner);

(viii) disqualification (from driving);

(ix)   fine (for indictable offences any fine can be imposed unless a statute prescribes a special maximum; summary offences are grouped into five categories, each carrying its own maximum penalty which can be increased by an order of the Home Secretary to take account of inflation);

(x)   forfeiture of property used in the offence (for example, a gun or a motor car);

(xi)   compensation order (offender is ordered to pay money to his victim who has suffered personal or proprietary harm; such an order may be made additional to, or instead of, any other sentence);

(xii) restitution order (stolen goods can be ordered to be returned to the person entitled to recover them);

(xiii) criminal bankruptcy order (where the victim has sustained loss or damage exceeding £15,000);

(xiv) binding over (the offender is bound over to keep the peace or be of good behaviour; he is required to furnish a recognisance which is, in effect, a suspended fine);

(xv) conditional discharge (the offender is discharged but this is conditional upon his not offending again within three years);

(xvi) absolute discharge (despite conviction, the offender is not punished as such; this would occur where the offence was trivial or if the conviction were only 'technical').

Courts have the power to defer sentencing for up to six months; they also have the power to impose an 'extended sentence' upon a dangerous offender (see pages 183–4).

The above sentences are generally available when sentencing young adults (aged between seventeen and twenty-one) with two major exceptions. First, no custodial sentence for a young adult can be suspended. Secondly, the provision for custodial sentences for such persons is somewhat different, the philosophy being that they should not be imprisoned alongside hardened adult criminals. Young adults and 'young persons' (aged fourteen to sixteen) can receive short custodial sentences of between twenty-one days and four months in the form of 'detention centre orders' where the emphasis is on a rigorous regime of physical exercise, work and education. Where a sentence of longer than four months is thought to be appropriate, the young adult (or young person aged fifteen or sixteen) must be sentenced to a specified period of youth custody to be served at a youth custody centre (formerly borstals). If a young adult aged eighteen to twenty-one is convicted of murder or other offence carrying a maximum penalty of life imprisonment and the court feels custody for life is appropriate, it must sentence him to 'custody for life' which is usually served in prison (similar provision for indeterminate detention for juveniles exists under section 53 of the Children and Young Persons Act 1933, as amended).

With regard to 'mentally disordered' offenders (a technical term, defined by the Mental Health Act 1983), the same range of penalties is available as for all adult offenders – with psychiatric probation orders being of special importance. Additionally, however, the courts have power to make a hospital or a guardianship order which results in the offender being compulsorily received into guardianship or a hospital – which may be one of four 'special', secure hospitals or an ordinary National Health Service hospital. (Since 1984 a limited number of places in Secure Units has been provided by Regional Health Authorities.)

The sentencing judge, having selected the type of sentence, also has considerable discretion as to the length of that sentence. Statutes specifying terms of imprisonment are laying down maxima. Theft, for instance, carries a maximum of ten years' imprisonment. The judge can impose *any* period of imprisonment up to this maximum (or, of course, any other type of sentence). It ought to be borne in mind that all sentences of imprisonment are cut by one-third remission for good conduct and that prisoners can be released on parole after serving one third of their sentence or six months' imprisonment, whichever is the longer.

It is thus clear that tremendous discretionary power is vested in the sentencing judge. Which sentence he chooses, and its length, depends very much on what he sees the purposes of punishment and the criminal law to be. It is to this issue that the final section of this book will be primarily devoted.

Finally, it is crucial to stress (and it is very much a theme of this book) that not only judges are influenced by the purposes of punishment and the criminal law when sentencing convicted defendants. These concerns have also been of prime importance in the shaping of the substantive criminal law. The rules of the criminal law (the 'substantive' law) and the punishment of offenders are the two sides of the same coin. A whole range of substantive issues, for example whether offences of strict liability are justifiable or how the boundaries of the law of attempt or conspiracy should be drawn, are, in reality, issues about whether punishment is justified in such cases and would help achieve the purposes of the criminal law. It is to these substantive issues that we now turn.

2

Constructing Criminal Liability

A. INTRODUCTION

The criminal law sets standards that largely reflect community values of what is wrong and harmful. For instance, few would disagree that murder, rape and theft are such wrongs. By setting these standards and punishing those who do not conform to them, law-makers hope to strengthen respect for the standards and to encourage people to comply with them.

In laying down such standards the criminal law is faced with two central problems. First, what are the community values so important that they need to be enforced by the criminal law (as opposed to other mechanisms of social control – say, education, morality or religion)? For example, is sniffing glue or selling pornographic books the sort of activity we want to *punish* using the criminal law, or should we simply try to educate people into not participating in such activities? Discussion of this first point will be reserved until later when the broader issue of the function of the criminal law is examined. Secondly, the law must define proscribed activities (crimes) with some precision. It must be specific about the standards it is laying down. To say that murder is, and ought to be, a crime begs the question: in what circumstances is killing to be treated as murder? The surgeon who performs a dangerous operation on his patient might well 'kill' that patient (that is, the operation could be the cause of the patient's death), but if the operation were performed under proper conditions by a surgeon trying to save the life of his patient, one would clearly not wish to punish the surgeon. Or, putting it another way, the law must define murder (and other homicide offences) in such a manner as to exclude the surgeon from its ambit.

The problem is one of defining the circumstances in which a particular crime is committed. Let us take the example of rape: should this crime cover the man who genuinely believes the woman is consenting to sexual intercourse when in fact she is not? Should it encompass the man who has intercourse with a woman who is so drunk she is unaware of what is happening? And should it be rape to persist in intercourse with a woman who initially consented to penetration but, mid-way through the intercourse, changes her mind?

Every crime raises its own particular problems of definition. For instance, issues relating to vaginal penetration are unique to the crime of rape. Nevertheless, most crimes do raise broadly the same general issues – for example, should it be a crime accidentally to cause a harm; should it be criminal to cause a harm if one genuinely thinks one is not causing any harm (say, because one has made a mistake and thinks one's 'victim' is consenting); should it be criminal to try to commit a crime, or simply to plan a crime, when no ultimate harm occurs; should it be criminal to cause a harm deliberately if one thought it was necessary to do so to save one's own life; in what circumstances can someone be said to have 'caused' a harm? The answers to these and other similar fundamental questions are often called 'the general principles of criminal liability' – the basic rules for constructing criminal liability.

Traditionally, the basic rule has been expressed in the Latin maxim: *actus non facit reum nisi mens sit rea* ('an act does not made a man guilty of a crime unless his mind is also guilty' – per Lord Hailsham in *Haughton v. Smith*, 1975). Thus before criminal liability can be imposed, the law generally insists upon proof of two elements:

1. *Actus reus*: certain conduct by the defendant. This conduct can be simply forbidden in itself (for example, possessing a firearm contrary to section 1 of the Firearms Act 1968). Such crimes are known as 'conduct crimes'. But more usually, particularly with serious crimes, the conduct must cause a forbidden consequence (for example, pulling the trigger of a loaded gun and thereby killing the victim). Such crimes are known as 'result crimes'.

2. *Mens rea*: a blameworthy state of mind (for example, intending to kill the victim when discharging the gun).

These two elements must coincide in time. The defendant must have the necessary *mens rea* at the moment he commits the *actus reus*; it is not sufficient that he had *mens rea* before or after the *actus reus*. Thus if a defendant accidentally discharges his gun, killing the victim, there is no *mens rea* at the time of the *actus reus*. If that defendant, not realising that he has already killed the victim, then decides to murder him and shoots the corpse, there can be no liability for murder. The *mens rea* (intending to kill) did not coincide with the *actus reus* (killing the victim). The law is, however, prepared to adopt a flexible approach in this regard by holding that in certain cases there can be a 'continuing *actus reus*' and all that is necessary is that *mens rea* exist at any stage during this extended *actus reus*. In *Thabo Meli* (1954) the defendants, in accordance with a prearranged plan, struck their victim over the head in a hut. Believing him to be dead, they took his body to a cliff and rolled it over. In fact the man was not dead, but died of exposure while unconscious at the foot of the cliff. It was argued that the *actus reus* (the act that caused death) was rolling the body over the cliff and at that time the defendants had no *mens rea* as they thought they were disposing of a corpse. This argument was rejected, on the ground that what had occurred was 'one series of acts' and that as the defendants had had *mens rea* at some stage during this series of acts (when they struck their victim in the hut) the necessary coincidence of *actus reus* and *mens rea* had been established; the defendants were guilty of murder.

These two general prerequisites, *actus reus* and *mens rea*, are not required for every crime. In particular, many crimes can be committed without *mens rea*, namely the so-called crimes of strict liability. Further, and this point must be stressed at this stage, these two prerequisities vary greatly from crime to crime in the precise form they take. For the crime of attempt, for instance, it must be proved that the defendant acted with intent to commit the full offence whereas for other crimes, such as criminal damage, it is sufficient to establish that he acted recklessly. In other words, both the *actus reus* and *mens rea* requirements have a chameleon-like quality in that they change their colours from crime to crime – particularised fine-tuning with regard to their precise meanings is necessary in relation to each particular offence.

23

These Latin terms, *actus reus* and *mens rea*, have been condemned by Lord Diplock in the House of Lords in *Miller* (1983) as being unhelpful and confusing terminology. Indeed, they are more than this: they are positively misleading for two main reasons. First, the Latin maxim suggests that if the forbidden harm is produced by a defendant acting with a guilty state of mind, criminal liability will inevitably ensue. This is clearly not always the case. For instance, a defendant might intentionally kill another but escape all criminal liability because he has a defence, such as self-defence. Or, despite having the requisite *mens rea* for murder, he might instead be convicted of the lesser offence of manslaughter because he has a partial defence, such as provocation. Such defences cannot be naturally accommodated within the language of *actus reus* and *mens rea*. Consequently divergent interpretations have emerged as to how the constituent elements of a crime should be defined employing the orthodox terminology. One view is that there are, in reality, three ingredients of a crime: *actus reus, mens rea* and the absence of a valid defence. On the other hand, it can be argued that there are only the two basic components of a crime, *actus reus* and *mens rea*, but that the existence of a defence negates either the *actus reus* or the *mens rea*. However, the problem with all these interpretations is that they tend to obscure the real issue which is simply one of determining who *ought* to be brought within the ambit of the criminal law, and at what level (for example, murder or manslaughter). While it is often useful to analyse crimes in terms of *actus reus* and *mens rea*, the true construction of criminal liability cannot be made dependent on any artificial and rigid classification.

The second reason for departing from the traditional analysis is that the terms *actus reus* and *mens rea* have, over the years, so changed their meaning that these original descriptions do not accurately reflect the reality of the law. For instance, the orthodox view is that *mens rea* denotes a mental element. We shall see that English law commonly deems a defendant to have *mens rea* if he fails to consider an obvious and serious risk. It is highly artificial and unhelpful to describe the absence of a state of mind (failing to consider the risk) as a state of mind. While recognising that a familiarity with the orthodox terminology is essential to a true understanding of the criminal law (and is therefore necessarily preserved in much of this book), these problems associated with the concepts *actus reus* and *mens rea* suggest that an attempt should be made to construct criminal liability in terms that do reflect the reality of the law. What, then, is this reality?

The criminal law generally seeks to punish those who are *blameworthy in causing harm* – and the level of punishment meted out will reflect the degree of blame or fault to be attached to their conduct as well as reflecting the extent of the harm they have caused. In many cases, of course, the reason why we blame someone for their conduct is because of their state of mind at the time of that conduct. Thus we blame a defendant who *deliberately* strikes his victim and knocks him down a flight of stairs. If that defendant had instead tripped on a badly fitted carpet on the stairs and accidentally fallen into the victim knocking him down the same stairs, our moral assessment of the event would be quite different. We would not blame this latter defendant, and, accordingly, would generally not seek to punish him. So, in many cases, the presence or absence of a particular state of mind (*mens rea*) in the defendant can indicate whether or not we blame him for his actions. But traditional *mens rea* is no more than an *indicator* of blame. We can sometimes blame a person who does not act with *mens rea*. If our hypothetical defendant had consumed an excessive amount of alcohol or drugs and, while staggering drunkenly down the stairs, had unwittingly knocked the victim down, our response might be: he *ought* to have noticed the victim; he *ought* not to have rendered himself so intoxicated that he became unaware of his surroundings and his actions; we *blame* him for getting so intoxicated that he caused harm to the victim.

Further, we do not blame all persons who act with *mens rea*. A defendant might intentionally cause a harm yet not be blamed because he had a valid justification or excuse for his actions. For instance, if the 'victim' on the stairs had been about to stab our defendant, we would regard the latter as being free from blame when he took defensive action and deliberately pushed the 'victim' down the stairs.

Thus it appears clear that while *mens rea* is often important in assessing blame, the two concepts are quite distinct – and it is blame that lies at the foundation of the construction of criminal liability. But, before examining this and the other basic concepts in more detail, one final introductory point needs to be made. We do not blame people for what they are. We do not blame someone for being ill or insane. We blame people for what they have done; we blame them for their *conduct*. If this conduct, committed in circumstances in which we can fairly blame the defendant, has caused a forbidden harm (or, in some cases, is regarded as a wrong or a harm in itself) we feel justified in imposing criminal liability and punishing the actor. Accordingly, it is possible at this stage to provide a working definition for the construction of criminal liability for most crimes – and one that particularly covers the more serious 'result-crimes': *criminal liability is imposed upon a blameworthy actor whose conduct has caused a forbidden harm*. For 'conduct crimes' a broadly similar definition suffices: *criminal liability is imposed upon a blameworthy actor whose conduct constitutes the forbidden harm*.

We are now in a position to examine the various elements in this definition in more detail to expose the precise meaning of these concepts and to explain when and how they apply in the criminal law.

B. CONDUCT

1. Necessity for Conduct

Criminal liability cannot be imposed on a defendant unless he has 'acted' – unless there is conduct. English law does not punish for 'thought-crime'. No matter how evil a person's thoughts and intentions, the law insists on a physical manifestation of such intention before it will intervene. There are several reasons for this insistence on conduct as a prerequisite of criminal liability. In evidential terms, it would be extremely difficult to base criminal liability purely on a defendant's evil intentions. Without conduct as corroboration, how could one ever prove that such evil thoughts existed? How could one differentiate between daydreams and fixed intentions? Also, evil

intentions, by themselves, are not regarded as sufficiently dangerous to justify the intervention of the law; the mental decision might
be too irresolute ever to be translated into action. Mere mental
decisions to commit crimes pose no threat in themselves to society;
they do not infringe other people's rights to security – thus no
identifiable harm exists for the criminal law to punish. And finally,
it would be an intolerable invasion of liberty and privacy for the law
to try to punish mere thoughts. Only when those thoughts are con-
verted into action is the law justified in intervening. The requirement of conduct helps preserve the liberty of the individual by
limiting criminal liability as much as possible.

2. Extent of Conduct

The exact type and amount of conduct required varies from crime to
crime. For most crimes there must be sufficient conduct to constitute
the prohibited wrong (for example, actually possessing controlled
drugs which is an offence contrary to the Misuse of Drugs Act 1971),
or sufficient conduct to produce the harmful result (for example, for
murder the defendant must do all those acts necessary to cause the
death of the victim).

However, for certain other crimes, the law is satisfied by a lesser
physical manifestation of the defendant's criminal intention. Let us
consider how much conduct is required in four such areas of criminal
law: attempt; conspiracy; incitement; and aiding, abetting, counselling and procuring.

(a) ATTEMPT

With an attempt to commit a crime, the defendant has not produced
the forbidden harm, but must have tried to do so. For instance, with
attempted murder the victim has not been killed but the defendant
must have made an effort to murder him. It is not enough that he
has decided to commit the crime. The law, as explained, insists on
conduct – a physical manifestation of a decision. The problem is to
establish *how much* conduct is necessary before it can be said there
has been an attempt to commit the crime.

Take, for instance, the famous case of *Robinson* (1915) where a jeweller, intending to defraud his insurance company, hid all his insured jewellery, tied himself up and called for help, representing to the police that his premises had been burgled. The police discovered the truth and the jeweller was charged with attempting to obtain money from the insurers by false pretences. This was a case where there was a clearly proved intention to commit the crime, and the defendant had 'acted' – he had certainly taken some steps towards the commission of the crime. The Court of Criminal Appeal, however, held that the jeweller had not done enough to be liable for the attempt. His acts were 'only remotely connected with the commission of the full offence, and not immediately connected with it' (citing Baron Parke in *Eagleton*, 1855). Not only will the law allow one to plan crimes in the privacy of one's own head, but it will also permit one to *prepare* for the commission of that crime. The jeweller's acts were only such 'mere preparation'. Only when a defendant has proceeded *beyond the stage of preparation* will the law seek to intervene.

Such reasoning has been confirmed by section 1 (1) of the Criminal Attempts Act 1981 which provides that in order to be guilty of an attempt to commit an offence a person must have done 'an act which is more than merely preparatory to the commission of the offence'.

We have examined why the law demands some conduct. But why does it insist on so much conduct? Why does the law not punish purely preparatory acts? After all, when a person has started preparing for his crime we are able to overcome the evidential problem of not being able to prove 'mere intentions'; his actions now demonstrate some firmness of purpose; arguments concerning invasion of liberty and privacy become less plausible when a person has actually committed physical actions directed towards the commission of a crime; and, of course, imposing liability for preparatory acts would allow the police to intervene at an earlier stage to prevent the commission of crimes. Such reasoning led the Law Commission in 1973 to propose that liability for attempt should be imposed at the much earlier stage when the defendant had merely taken a 'substantial step' towards the commission of his crime (Law Commission, 1973). For example, a person 'reconnoitring the place contemplated for the commission of the intended offence' or 'preparing or acting a falsehood for the purpose of an offence of fraud or deception', which would cover the jeweller in *Robinson* (1915), would be liable for attempt under such a proposal.

Such thinking reflects what can be described as a 'subjectivist' approach to the law of attempt. This approach, while insisting on *some* conduct as corroboration of the defendant's purpose, nevertheless stresses the mental element of the defendant. He intended to commit a crime; he is dangerous and needs restraining; he also needs rehabilitation and punishment to deter him and others from attempting to commit crimes. Criminal liability can thus justifiably be imposed at a much earlier stage.

However, while English law has embraced a subjectivist approach in many other areas of the criminal law (including impossible attempts: see pages 109–13), it has here preferred the view that liability in such cases would involve too serious an invasion of personal liberty; it would open the door to the possibility of abuse by the police and 'goes much too far in making guilty intention overshadow guilty conduct' (Law Commission, 1980). Also, the mere preparer is regarded as relatively non-dangerous. Only when he has got sufficiently near to committing the crime that he can be said to have 'broken through the psychological barrier to crime' (Glanville Williams, 1978) or to have 'crossed the Rubicon and burnt his boats' (*DPP v. Stonehouse*, 1978) can he be regarded as sufficiently dangerous to warrant restraining. In short, English law can be said to have adopted an 'objectivist' approach to defining the contours of this aspect of the law of attempt. An objectivist approach focuses on the *actions* of the defendant; these actions must 'conform to objective criteria defined in advance. The act must evidence attributes subject to determination independently of the actor's intent' (Fletcher, 1978). In the law of attempt the defendant's actions must bring him 'within striking distance' of committing the crime. Only at this point does his conduct generate apprehension; only then does it present a clear threat of harm justifying the imposition of criminal liability.

English law used to translate this requirement as one of 'proximity' – the defendant's actions must be proximate to the complete crime. However, as the literal meaning of 'proximate' is 'nearest, next before or after' (Law Commission, 1980), a 'proximity test' would seem to indicate that the defendant must have done the *final act* left for him to do. Robinson, for example, would need to have actually filed his insurance claim; the would-be assassin would need to have actually pulled the trigger of his gun. Wishing to extend attempt liability beyond such limited cases, while still maintaining an overall objectivist orientation, the Criminal Attempts Act 1981, section 1(1), abandoned the common law language of 'proximity' and, instead, simply insisted that the person's conduct be 'more than merely preparatory to the commission of the offence'.

It is still an open question whether section 1 (1) has in fact shifted the boundaries of the law of attempt. In *Boyle and Boyle* (1987) it was stated that reference to the tests applied before 1981 is permissible. The recent decision in *Gullefer* (1987) suggests that the Act has pushed back the boundaries of the law of attempt in that the 'Rubicon test' appears to have been abandoned: a defendant need not have reached a point of no return. But even if he has reached such a point he will not necessarily be liable. For instance, the jeweller in *Robinson* (1915) had probably 'crossed the Rubicon and burnt his boats' when he called for help and represented to the police that his premises had been burgled. It nevertheless remains that he was still only at the pre-paratory stage. To prepare for his crime he had to hide his jewellery and persuade the police that he had been robbed. Only then would he be in a position, beyond preparation, to start committing his crime – by making his claim to the insurance company. On this basis it seems likely that an act is only more than merely preparatory when the defendant is in the process of committing the intended offence – when he has 'embarked on the crime proper' (*Gullefer*, 1987). It follows that *Robinson* (1915) and other similar common law cases could well be decided in the same way today. Whether this would actually be so, however, now largely depends upon the jury. Under the Criminal Attempts Act 1981, section 4(3), it is for the judge to decide as a matter of law whether the defendant's actions *could* amount to an attempt, but, if so, it is for the jury to decide, as a matter of fact, whether they *did* so amount to an attempt. It is thus possible that two different juries could reach different verdicts today if faced with the facts of *Robinson* (1915).

(b) CONSPIRACY

While fairly substantial action is required for an attempt, all that is required for a conspiracy is an agreement between at least two persons to commit a crime (Criminal Law Act 1977, section 1(1); section 5 of this Act also preserves two species of common law conspiracy, namely, conspiracy to defraud – section 5 (2) – and conspiracy to corrupt public morals or outrage public decency – section 5 (3)). The essence of the crime is the agreement itself; if this can be proved, no further conduct is required. Thus if two persons agree to rob a bank they are guilty of a criminal conspiracy as soon as they have reached an agreement. This is not punishing 'evil thoughts' alone. Consistent with the general principle, there must be a physical manifestation of the evil intention – but here this requirement is satisfied merely by proof of an agreement (*Mulcahy*, 1868).

The real issue is whether such minimal conduct as a mere agreement to commit a crime *ought* to suffice for criminal liability. The rationale of 'nipping crime in the bud' is insufficient here. Such arguments apply with equal force to attempts, yet to be liable for an attempt, we have seen that the jeweller in *Robinson* (1915) would need to have done a great deal towards the actual commission of his crime. Why would he have been liable for conspiracy (and liable now to the same punishment as for the attempt) if he and another had simply agreed to defraud the insurers and had done nothing in pursuance of that agreement?

Two main arguments are usually put forward to justify the law of conspiracy. First, it is asserted that collaborations between persons or groups increase the dangerousness of their actions. The shared commitment to perpetrating the crime makes it more likely that the crime will actually be committed by at least one of the parties. And it is more difficult for society to protect itself against collective criminal agreements, say, by organised crime, than against the antisocial designs of an individual. Thus greater apprehension is generated by criminal agreements; they pose more of a threat to society. Under the objectivist view of the criminal law discussed above, an individual must come close to committing his crime before society is threatened, but the requisite threshold of threat and apprehension is crossed, both psychologically and practically, at a much earlier stage by a criminal agreement.

The second justification is that conspiracies may be regarded as more serious than attempts where there is an agreement to commit a series of offences. For instance, a crime network might be set up to organise the importation and distribution of prohibited drugs on a massive scale – and involving hundreds of persons. Such a collective criminal agreement is in itself far more serious and dangerous than any one isolated attempt to import drugs into the country. A conspiracy charge, revealing the larger criminal enterprise, will more accurately reflect the gravity of the conduct.

Whether such considerations are sufficient to justify punishing a mere agreement is an open question. In the USA many states insist upon an overt act in pursuance of the criminal agreement; one of the conspirators must actually do something towards committing the crime. While English law does not insist upon such a requirement, the fact remains that a mere agreement is almost impossible to prove unless some overt act has been performed from which the agreement can be inferred. But this point in fact exposes the law of conspiracy to yet another objection. We shall see later that the *mens rea* of most crimes can only be established by drawing inferences from acts; with conspiracy the *actus reus*, the agreement, can similarly be established by inference only in most cases. This means that conspiracy is completely a crime of inference – hardly a satisfactory state of affairs.

In many of the conspiracy cases, either the complete crime has actually been committed, or the overt acts relied upon as evidence of the agreement could well amount to attempts. In *Knuller* (1972) Lord Diplock stated that while a mere agreement did technically suffice for a conspiracy, in reality it was the overt acts done in concert that were truly dangerous and merited punishment. If this is so, one is left wondering whether a law of conspiracy is really necessary. The overt acts done in pursuance of a criminal agreement could well be dealt with by the law of attempt. If necessary, and particularly if the 'dangerousness of collaboration' argument were accepted, the boundaries of the law of attempt could be pushed back to cover some preparatory actions when dealing with group criminality. Such a proposal would ensure that a *significant* physical manifestation of a criminal intention was a necessary prerequisite to the imposition of criminal liability.

(c) INCITEMENT

The crime of incitement is a common law offence punishable on indictment with a fine and imprisonment at the discretion of the court. The essence of this offence is that the defendant must persuade, encourage or command another to commit a crime. The only 'conduct' required is words or actions of persuasion. In *Fitzmaurice* (1983) it was held that the necessary 'element of persuasion' was satisfied by a 'suggestion, proposal or request [that] was accompanied by an implied promise of reward'. If the person incited agrees to commit the offence, both are liable for conspiracy. If the incitee actually commits the crime, the incitor will be liable as an accessory to the complete offence – a point to be canvassed in the next section.

So, like conspiracy but unlike attempt, the actions of an incitor are far removed from the complete crime, making it questionable whether this offence has not pushed back the threshold of criminal liability too far. Why should mere words of persuasion involve criminal liability – particularly if nothing is done pursuant to those words? Are such words or actions manifestly dangerous? The incitee can, after all, resist such persuasion.

The justifications for the imposition of criminal liability upon such minimal conduct are similar to those already canvassed for the other inchoate offences, particularly conspiracy. The offence of incitement is necessary for timely police intervention to 'nip the crime in the bud'. An incitor has, by the fact of his incitement, indicated some degree of dangerousness; it is desirable to deter people from encouraging others to commit crime. Indeed, incitement can be seen as particularly dangerous because it may lead to more intelligent and careful planning and cooperation than if the hireling had simply acted on his own initiative. And finally, there is a view, not applicable to conspiracy, that the crime of incitement exists, in part at least, to protect the person incited from corruption (Gordon, 1978).

Whether these justifications are sufficiently convincing is a moot point. If the person incited agrees to commit the crime, there will be a criminal conspiracy; incitement thus amounts to no more than an attempted conspiracy – an offence expressly abolished by section 1(4) of the Criminal Attempts Act 1981. If the incitement is successful and the crime ultimately committed, it is easy to understand why the incitor's actions should be punished – his actions would have contributed significantly to the ultimate commission of the crime. In such cases, however, the crime of incitement is redundant: the incitor would clearly be liable as a counsellor or procurer of the offence under the rules of accessorial liability. On the other hand, if the incitement fails and does not even mature into a conspiracy, the imposition of criminal liability for such minimal conduct does seem contrary to the general spirit of the law which normally requires fairly extensive action as a prerequisite for the imposition of criminal liability.

(d) ACCESSORIES

An accessory (or accomplice or secondary party) is a person who helps or encourages another (the principal offender) to commit a crime. Section 8 of the Accessories and Abettors Act 1861 provides: 'whosoever shall aid, abet, counsel or procure the commission of any indictable offence . . . shall be liable to be tried, indicted and punished as a principal offender.'

The term 'aid and abet' is generally thought to cover an accessory who is present at the scene of the crime – although 'presence' must be liberally interpreted so as to cover, for example, the look-out or the get-away driver. 'Counsel' and 'procure', on the other hand, cover assistance or encouragement prior to the commission of the crime. With counselling there will normally have been a meeting of minds between the parties; this need not be so with procuring.

As section 8 makes clear, an accessory, of whichever type, is liable to the same extent as the principal offender (and so can be punished to the same extent) – despite the fact that he has not himself directly committed the crime. For instance, in *Craig and Bentley* (1952) Bentley, who was in police custody, called out to Craig, 'Let him have it.' Craig shot and killed a policeman and was convicted of murder but escaped the death penalty because of his youth. Bentley, because of his encouragement, was also convicted of murder; he, however, was hanged. The question for us to consider here is: how much conduct by an accessory is necessary to justify the imposition of criminal liability; how much help or encouragement must an accessory like Bentley give?

Consistent with the general principle, there must be some *conduct* by the accessory. His actions must amount to aiding, abetting, counselling or procuring the commission of the offence:

(i) Aiding and abetting: How much conduct is required by an accessory present at the scene of the crime? The answer here depends largely on whether the accessory is present at the crime as a result of a prior agreement or not. If he is, it follows that a criminal law prepared to punish mere agreements must be prepared to punish any overt acts done in pursuance of that agreement when those acts lead to the ultimate harm. Mere presence at the scene of the crime, pursuant to such a prior agreement, is sufficient conduct. Where there is a shared joint enterprise, each member of the group, even though his particular actions are minimal, assumes responsibility for the actions of the other members of that group. However, one is only a 'member of the group' when the group is acting in furtherance of a common purpose. If one of the parties departs completely from the concerted action of the common design, the other parties are no longer responsible for his actions.

In *Anderson and Morris* (1966) there was a 'common enterprise' between Anderson and Morris to engage in a fist fight with their victim, Welch. Anderson produced a knife and killed Welch with it. By departing so radically from the agreed joint enterprise, Anderson was effectively acting on his own and Morris escaped liability. If, on the other hand, Anderson had killed Welch with a blow from the fist, Morris would have been liable (for either murder or manslaughter depending on his *mens rea*); this would have been an action *within* the joint enterprise and Morris, even though he struck no blow, would be responsible for such an 'authorised act'. Thus in *Reid* (1975) Reid and two other defendants went to a man's house armed with guns; Reid did not expect the guns to be used. One of the other defendants shot and killed the victim when he answered the door. It was held that the joint enterprise was 'unlawful possession of offensive weapons' with intent to cause 'fright by threats to use them'. The death of the victim flowed directly from this common enterprise. The victim had been shot by one of the guns; it was the same as if Welch had been killed by a fist blow. Reid, although he had merely stood there and done nothing further himself, was responsible for the actions of the others and found liable. (Because he had not anticipated death, he was only liable for manslaughter.)

What is the position where no prior agreement or common purpose exists, but the defendant happens to be at the scene of the crime? In *Allan* (1965) the defendant witnessed his friends committing a crime (an affray, which involves unlawful fighting). He had a secret intention to join in if his help was needed, but he outwardly did nothing and simply played the role of a passive spectator. It was held that he could not be liable as he had not actually encouraged the participants. To have convicted him would have been getting uncomfortably close to convicting a person purely on the basis of his thoughts.

However, while some conduct is necessary, it is clear that the very slightest act of assistance or encouragement will suffice. In *Clarkson* (1971) the defendants entered a room in an army barracks where a woman was being raped. They remained there watching the rape. It was held that their mere presence, even if that presence gave encouragement, was not in itself sufficient. There had to be 'encouragement in fact' – this could consist of 'expressions, or gestures, or actions' signifying approval or encouragement. So if the defendants in *Allan* (1965) and *Clarkson* (1971) had cheered, clapped or shouted encouragement, this 'conduct' could have been sufficient to render them criminally liable.

If one recalls the law of attempt where very substantial conduct is required, one is forced to ask: why is such minimal conduct as shouting encouragement sufficient for accessorial liability? One possible explanation is that even such minor assistance can 'strengthen the resolve of the perpetrator' (Fletcher, 1978); it can give him the necessary fortitude to continue with the offence. We all know from our everyday experiences that we are sometimes prepared to take risks with the support of another that we are unprepared to take alone. Assistance or encouragement can thus increase the possibility of the offence occurring. While this can clearly be so in some cases, it hardly seems a plausible general explanation. The rapists in *Clarkson* (1971) appeared well committed to their rape and it is doubtful whether words or gestures of encouragement from Clarkson would have had any impact or effect at all.

Further, this idea presupposes that the principal offender is aware of the encouragement or assistance he is receiving, and is thus capable of having his resolve strengthened. Yet in *Quick and Paddison* (1973) it was held that an accessory could assist a principal who was unaware of such assistance, a view endorsed by the Law Commission (Law Commission, 1985).

Another view is that here, unlike the law of attempt, the actual harm has been caused. The policeman in *Craig and Bentley* (1952) was dead; the girl in *Clarkson* (1971) was raped. The question is one of deciding who should bear the responsibility for such a harm. Clearly many accessories ought to be held accountable because their actions may have contributed to the result. Craig might have fired his gun only because of the shouted encouragement from Bentley. In other cases the actions of the accessory may have enabled the principal to commit the offence more easily or safely. Even though they are minimal actions, if they contribute to, or facilitate, the ultimate commission of the crime, the accessory (assuming, of course, he has *mens rea*) ought to be held responsible. Even if one accepts this argument, however, one must still ask whether an accessory, who has done so little, ought to be held responsible *for the same offence* as the principal. Assuming his contribution is not so great as to amount to a legal cause of the ultimate harm, should an accessory not be punished for the harm he has actually caused, namely, the harm of assisting or encouraging the principal offender? Bentley did not himself kill anyone. Did he deserve to be found guilty of murder? We clearly blame him for encouraging Craig to kill. Should he not have been punished for *what he did*, namely, that encouragement – which, presumably, would be a lesser criminal offence involving less punishment?

(ii) Counselling and procuring. How much conduct is required by an accessory who is not present at the scene of the crime? Typically, counselling refers to advice, information, encouragement or the supply of tools prior to the commission of a crime. For instance, in *Bainbridge* (1960) the defendant was liable because he supplied oxygen-cutting equipment to the principal offender who used it to break into premises. The requisite conduct can even be normal action in

the course of a lawful business. For example, in *National Coal Board v. Gamble* (1959) a purchaser loaded his lorry with coal and had it weighed to ascertain the cost. On weighing the coal the weighbridge operator pointed out to the purchaser that the lorry was overloaded. The purchaser said he would risk it, whereupon the operator gave him the weight ticket enabling the purchaser to leave the colliery. This act was held to be a sufficient 'positive act of assistance' to render the weighbridge operator (and thus the National Coal Board as his employer) liable as an accessory to the crime of driving an overweight lorry on the road. On this basis if a shopkeeper sold an alarm clock knowing it was to be used for constructing a time-bomb, he would become an accessory to the offence committed by the bomber. Despite the fact that the principal offender could have obtained the alarm clock anywhere, the fact remains that the accessory has supplied an 'essential article' to the commission of the crime (*National Coal Board v. Gamble*, 1959).

Procuring, on the other hand, refers to an accessory who instigates a crime: 'To procure means to produce by endeavour. You procure a thing by setting out to see that it happens and taking the appropriate steps to produce that happening' (*Attorney-General's Reference, No. 1 of 1975*). Thus a defendant who surreptitiously laces his friend's drinks with double measures of spirits knowing his friend is about to drive his car home is liable for procuring the offence of drunken driving committed by the friend.

Again, with both counselling and procuring the defendant's actual conduct can be fairly minimal. In relation to procuring this is not difficult to justify. The procurer is the instigator. His actions are significant; they are a cause (and, perhaps, the decisive cause) of the prohibited result. Indeed, it has been stated that one cannot procure an offence unless there is a causal link between that procuring and the commission of the offence (*Attorney General's Reference No. 1 of 1975*). Many cases of counselling, too, involve such instigation, clearly justifying the imposition of criminal liability – on the basis of the quality of the conduct, as opposed to the quantity. For instance, in *Richards* (1974), the defendant, Mrs Richards, employed two men to beat up her husband; her idea was that if he was seriously injured and in hospital for a month he would turn to her for love and affection! The two men duly attacked Mr Richards, wounding him. In this case Mrs Richards masterminded the whole crime and there is no problem justifying the imposition of criminal liability. Indeed, in some jurisdictions such as Germany, the actions of such instigators are regarded as more reprehensible than those of an accessory simply assisting the principal at the scene of the crime; their causal contribution towards the ultimate crime is certainly greater; the law thus provides for a higher level of punishment (Fletcher, 1978).

In England, however, the current view is that no distinction should be drawn between the level of liability and punishment of a principal offender and an accessory – and, in turn, as between accessories present at the crime and those not present (*Howe*, 1987). The extent of each party's liability will depend on his *mens rea* at the time of acting. This has always been the law in relation to aiders and abettors present at the crime but represents a change of direction in the law with regard to counsellors such as Mrs Richards who are not present. The older rule, established in *Richards* (1974), was that such counsellors could *not* be guilty of a more serious crime than the principal offender. Presumably, the rationale underlying the older approach was that, no matter how significant the conduct of the absent counsellor, he lacked control over the actual incident; his causal contribution was therefore weaker than that of the principal. Such distinctions have now been swept aside by the House of Lords in *Howe* (1987). Mrs Richards could now, because of her greater blameworthiness, be convicted of a greater offence than the principal offender just as if she had been present at the scene of the crime.

In other cases of counselling, however, the accessory's contribution need not be as significant. In *Calhaem* (1985) it was held that no causal connection was necessary for counselling as long as the offence committed was 'within the authority or advice' of the counsellor. In such cases the only rationale for punishing such minimal conduct is, again, that such advice or encouragement might have prompted the principal into action or strengthened his resolve. The supply of tools or advice might have had the same effect or made the commission of the crime easier or more certain. Further, with counselling there has been a meeting of minds. This can lead to momentum being gathered towards the commission of the crime and thus the same justifications as those underlying the law of conspiracy are applicable here.

But, again, the question raises itself: Why is the accessory punished for the same crime as that committed by the principal? Is such a form of derivative liability justifiable? Or, should the counsellor or procurer be punished for what he actually did, namely, encouraging or advising the commission of the crime? According to such reasoning the accessory's true fault and his danger to society reside in his actions of encouragement or assistance themselves. On this basis the accessory who instigated a crime would be guilty of the offence of incitement and a new offence of encouraging or assisting a crime would need to be created. There would, of course, be immense problems with such an approach: the new offence might need to be defined relative to the principal offence as, for example, encouraging murder is clearly worse than encouraging theft. However, the shift in focus would be desirable. Emphasis would be placed on the actual conduct of the defendant, and punishment geared to that (assuming, of course, he possessed *mens rea*) – rather than the present position where shouting words of encouragement can be deemed to be equal to pulling the trigger and killing a person.

3. Meaning of Conduct

(a) VOLUNTARY ACTS

The conduct or actions of the defendant must be 'voluntary'. For example, if a defendant is roughly pushed into the victim, knocking him over, the defendant's 'actions' are clearly involuntary – indeed, they are hardly *his* 'acts' at all. Similarly, if a sleeping mother, sharing a bed with her child, rolls over and smothers the child, her actions will be held to be involuntary. A person can be held responsible only for his voluntary actions. If his physical movements are involuntary, there will generally be no criminal liability. Not only would punishment be undeserved in such cases, but also it could serve no deterrent function – involuntary action clearly cannot be deterred.

The real problem, however, has been to define the term 'voluntary'. The traditional definition of a voluntary act is that it is 'a willed muscular contraction' (Holmes, 1881); it is a physical movement that results from an operation of the will. The mind is in control of bodily movements; it sends instructions to the muscles; the result is voluntary acts. Occasionally, however, the mind may not be in control of the body, and bodily movements may take place independently; such movements are involuntary acts: 'The mind is . . . [the controlling] agent, whereas the body alone is only a dumb brute – and, as everyone knows, it makes no sense at all to hold dumb brutes responsible' (Gross, 1979).

This orthodox definition is not particularly helpful. If we decide to do something, say, hit someone or open a door, our movements become coordinated to our goal. Of course, there are muscular movements but we are not aware of them at a conscious level; we do not have to 'instruct' our muscles to operate; such movements simply flow from our decision to act. And there is little point in arguing that the will must be controlling the muscles, albeit at a subconscious level – because this must also be true of many of the classical instances of involuntary conduct: the mother who rolled over in her sleep killing her child did not roll over because of the forces of gravity!

Hart (1968) has suggested that the criterion of voluntariness should be whether the movements were 'subordinated to the agent's conscious plans of action'; the issue would be whether they occurred 'as part of anything the agent takes himself to be doing'. If one means to open a door, then even though one is concentrating on something else, all physical movements geared towards opening the door are voluntary. But if, on the way to the door, one trips and, in falling, sticks out an arm to protect oneself, this movement of sticking out the arm would not be part of one's plan of action and would therefore be involuntary. Similarly, the mother rolling over in her sleep is clearly acting involuntarily; her movements are not any part of any action she means to take; she is unconscious and therefore does not take herself to be doing any action at all.

The criminal law, perhaps not surprisingly, has not truly attempted to face these complex problems. Instead, it has preferred to use the requirement of voluntariness as a mechanism to exclude a diverse range of cases from its ambit. It has, in effect, 'defined' voluntariness by example: some human conduct is simply perceived as too abnormal to be brought within the ambit of the criminal law.

Before considering some of these instances of involuntary conduct, or *automatism* as it is technically known, a crucial point must be borne in mind. In the classic case of involuntary conduct, such as the mother rolling over and smothering her child in her sleep, such automatism exempts the defendant completely from all criminal liability; she will walk out of court a free person. Being aware of this, the courts have done two things to prevent too many people escaping liability on the basis of automatism. First, they have tended to adopt a narrow interpretation of 'involuntariness' as the following list will reveal. And, secondly, they have tended to expand the definition of insanity so that some cases of classic automatism might now be regarded as cases of insanity. Where a defendant is found to be insane, he does not go free; he receives a special verdict – 'not guilty by reason of insanity' – and is subjected to mandatory commitment, namely, indefinite detention 'at Her Majesty's pleasure'. Using this device, control, either for incapacitative or rehabilitative purposes, can be maintained over the defendant.

The following cases are, or have been, traditionally thought to exclude voluntariness and thus give rise to a defence of automatism:

Physical compulsion: for example, if a person is knocked off a bicycle and lands on a pedestrian, the cyclist's actions are clearly involuntary and he cannot be liable for any injuries sustained by the pedestrian.

Reflex movements of external origin: in *Hill v. Baxter* (1958) it was stated that purely reflexive movements of the arms and legs caused by being attacked by a swarm of bees would not be voluntary. Such a person, for instance, could not be said to be 'driving' a car.

Concussion: a blow on the head or other physical trauma may sometimes produce a 'black-out' or 'confusional state', during which a person may engage in previously learned behaviour without being fully aware of what he is doing. While such a person is not completely unconscious, his ability to control his movements is sufficiently impaired to preclude criminal responsibility. His actions are deemed to be involuntary.

Unconsciousness: where the unconsciousness is 'normal', for example, our hypothetical case of the sleeping mother, or is externally caused as where a general anaesthetic is administered for therapeutic purposes, any physical movements are involuntary and will give rise to the complete defence of automatism. On the other hand, where the unconsciousness is the result of a neurophysiological disturbance such as a stroke or epilepsy, the position is more doubtful. Any physical movements in such a state are clearly equally involuntary, but as a result of the House of Lords decision of *Sullivan* (1983), there is a real chance that an insanity verdict might be returned. The effect of this decision is canvassed below.

Hypnosis: English law has not yet faced the problem of a defendant who commits a crime while under a hypnotic influence – although there are dicta indicating that such conduct would be involuntary (*Quick*, 1973). There is much scientific uncertainty as to the effect of hypnosis. There are claims, for instance, that one cannot hypnotise subjects to do acts they are unwilling to perform. Nevertheless, the view expressed in the Model Penal Code in the United States seems likely to prevail, namely, that 'the dependency and helplessness of the hypnotised subject are too pronounced' to justify the imposition of criminal liability.

Somnambulism: in one case a woman, dreaming her house was on fire, arose in a panic screaming 'save my children' and threw her baby out of the window (Walker, 1968). In the Australian case of *Cogdon* (1951) Mrs Cogdon, in a somnambulistic state, dreaming that her daughter was being attacked by ghosts, spiders and North Korean soldiers, axed her to death. She was acquitted on the ground that her actions were not voluntary. Despite the fact that the acts of a sleepwalker are not entirely purposeless, the link between mind and bodily action is too distorted to justify the imposition of criminal liability. The sleepwalker is not acting with his normal conscious mind. However, despite wide consensus on this point, the decision of *Sullivan* (1983) raises the possibility that sleepwalkers might be found 'not guilty by reason of insanity'.

Hypoglycaemia: hypoglycaemia is a deficiency of blood-sugar which can be caused when diabetics take insufficient food after insulin. This can lead to impaired functioning of the central nervous system which can cause confusion, poor coordination and, sometimes, aggressive behaviour. In *Quick* (1973) and *Bailey* (1983) it was held that a defendant could not truly be said to be acting voluntarily during a hypoglycaemic episode and so would generally be entitled to an acquittal on the basis of automatism. Again, in such cases there is now a risk after *Sullivan* (1983) that the special insanity verdict might have to be returned.

Epilepsy: if, during an epileptic fit, the defendant's spasms or physical convulsions cause injury to another, the generally accepted view was that there would be no criminal liability; automatism was the appropriate verdict. However, the House of Lords has now twice held that such a sufferer is, during his epileptic fit, *insane* (*Bratty*, 1963; *Sullivan*, 1983). A person who is legally insane can also be acting in an involuntary manner but is suffering from a 'disease of the mind'. In *Sullivan* (1983) the defendant, while recovering from an epileptic fit, attacked a friend and kicked him about the head and body. The House of Lords ruled that Sullivan's actions were caused by a disease of the mind; during his epileptic fit he was insane; it was irrelevant that the mental impairment was only temporary. The House indicated that an acquittal on grounds of automatism should be reserved for cases where the involuntary conduct was caused by 'some external factor such as a blow on the head causing concussion or the administration of an anaesthetic for therapeutic purposes'. Where the cause of the mental impairment was internal, as it clearly is with epilepsy, the insanity verdict was appropriate.

This decision is most unfortunate. One can, perhaps, understand the thinking behind the judgment. If the involuntary conduct has an internal cause, then it is likely to recur; society needs protection against the recurrence of such dangerous conduct – such protection cannot be achieved if the defendant is acquitted on grounds of automatism; the insanity verdict allows control to be maintained over the defendant. However, it seems absurd as well as highly insulting to epileptics to utilise the insanity verdict here. Nothing can be achieved by detaining such persons 'at Her Majesty's pleasure'. The reality is that most such persons will simply plead guilty to the charge, as Sullivan himself did, and will often receive a non-custodial sentence.

The *Sullivan* (1983) decision also has a potentially far-reaching effect on the other traditional areas of automatism. Our hypothetical sleeping mother would fortunately be unaffected by the *Sullivan* (1983) principle as simply rolling over in one's sleep, while not externally caused, could never be described as a 'mental impairment'. But somnambulism clearly does not have an external cause and *could* be regarded as resulting from some form of mental impairment. Nevertheless, it would plainly be a negation of common sense if sleepwalkers were to be regarded as insane – and the lower courts have been reluctant to take such an anomalous step. In *Lilienfield* (1985) a sleepwalker who stabbed his friend twenty times with a kitchen knife leaving him permanently paralysed was acquitted on the basis of automatism. Similarly, diabetics who suffer hypo-glycaemic episodes could well be regarded as insane under this test – unless it could be argued that failing to take food was an 'external factor'. Again, it is hoped that the courts will resist any temptation to characterise such diabetics as insane. Little would be achieved by what could only be regarded as a 'knee-jerk' classification.

It has been suggested that a distinction could be drawn between 'obviously non-purposive' conduct and actions that 'look purposive' (Glanville Williams, 1983; Smith, 1983). A spasm or convulsion while in the throes of an epileptic fit would be 'obviously non-purposive' and should result in an acquittal on grounds of automatism. On the other hand, Sullivan's conduct in kicking his friend 'looked purposive' – these were not convulsions. In *Bratty* (1963), the other House of Lords epilepsy case, the defendant took off a girl's stocking and strangled her with it – again, conduct that 'looked purposive'. The problem with this distinction, however, is that the conduct of Mrs Cogdon as she axed her daughter to death similarly 'looked purposive' – indeed, it was purposive *within the context of her dreams*.

Perhaps the best solution to such problems would be to regard all such cases as automatism (and not insanity) and to give the courts power to make appropriate orders, including the power to detain in hospital. For instance, in the old Scottish case of *HM Advocate* v. *Fraser* (1878) a sleepwalker was discharged on condition that he slept alone in future. Under section 37(3) of the Mental Health Act 1983 a magistrates' court has power to make a hospital order without recording a conviction provided the person is suffering from a major form of mental disorder and the court is satisfied that he did the act charged. A provision such as this, with suitable amendment, would enable the courts to give effect to the present proposal. In most cases of automatism (concussion etc.) there would be no need to make any kind of order. But giving the courts such power which could be utilised in cases such as *Bratty* (1963) and *Sullivan* (1983) would make it unnecessary for them to have to expand the concept of insanity to such an unacceptable extent in order to maintain some control over the defendant.

(b) DEEMED ACTS

Despite the basic rule that voluntary conduct is a necessary prerequisite to the imposition of criminal liability, in certain circumstances this requirement is waived or, at least, 'stretched' to a point where the law is simply 'deeming' a person to have acted voluntarily. This occurs in the following situations:

(i) Involuntary conduct preceded by fault. The criminal law is concerned with the punishment of the blameworthy. In most of the cases of involuntary conduct discussed above no blame can be laid at the defendant's door. It is generally not a person's fault that a blow to his head causes concussion or that he lashes out his arms during a nightmare. The requirement of voluntary conduct relieves such persons of responsibility. But if it was the defendant's own fault that brought on the involuntary conduct or the resultant harm, the law will not allow him to escape liability by sheltering behind the facade of automatism. Thus, even though a person's conduct might actually be involuntary at the time he caused the harm, he will nevertheless be held liable if it was his fault he got himself into that situation. One can view this in one of two ways. Either the defendant is being

punished for his voluntary conduct prior to the crime, or, because of the preceding fault, the requirement of voluntariness is dispensed with and he is simply deemed to have acted.

This principle is illustrated by the case of *Quick* (1973). The defendant, a diabetic, took his insulin but thereafter he ate hardly any food and consumed a quantity of alcohol. During the resultant hypoglycaemic episode he assaulted a victim. It was held that while hypoglycaemia could give rise to a defence of automatism, if the defendant was to blame for bringing about his condition he would be liable. It was stated that such a defendant is 'at fault' in bringing about his state of automatism when he does something (such as take a drug) or fails to do something (such as fail to eat after taking insulin) and he *knows*, or *ought to know*, that there is a risk of resultant involuntary conduct. In *Bailey* (1983) a diabetic ate insufficient food after a dose of insulin to combat its effect. It was held, rather surprisingly, that the risk of this leading to aggressive or unpredictable behaviour was not 'common knowledge, even among diabetics'. Accordingly, if the defendant could not be expected to know of these risks, he could not be blamed for any resultant involuntary conduct. Similarly, in *Hardie* (1984) it was held that a defendant who took Valium could escape liability for his subsequent involuntary conduct because it was not known to the defendant, nor generally known, that Valium could, in some cases, cause 'unpredictability or aggressiveness'. On the other hand, the risks involved in excessive consumption of other drugs (such as heroin or LSD) or alcohol are well known – accordingly, any defence of automatism would fail in such cases.

Such an approach inevitably leaves many questions unanswered. For instance, Mrs Cogdon had been sleepwalking in her daughter's room the very night previous to killing her and had awoken to find herself violently brushing dream-spiders off her daughter's face. She therefore knew of the risk that she would walk in her sleep – and would walk into her daughter's room; she even knew she could violently brush her daughter's face. Can we therefore blame her for axing her daughter to death the next night? What would be the true basis of such blame – that she knew she was a somnambulist, that she did not lock herself or her daughter up that night, or that she had not hidden her axe away (presumably there were knives or other instruments capable of being used against dream-North Koreans!)?

(ii) Status offences. Some crimes are defined in such a manner that there is no express requirement of conduct; the crime is committed when a certain state of affairs exists, or when the defendant is in a particular situation or condition or is of a defined, prohibited status. For instance, it is an offence simply to belong to a proscribed organisation such as the IRA (Prevention of Terrorism (Temporary Provisions) Act 1976, section 1(1)(a)). As this section covers those who joined prior to the date of commencement of the Act, it looks as though it is punishing the *mere status* of being a member of the IRA. However, consistent with the principle established in the preceding section, liability in such cases is justifiable (in terms of criminal law principles – whether such an offence ought to exist at all is another matter, discussed on pages 166–77) if it was the defendant's fault that the prohibited status or state of affairs has come about. For example, closer inspection of the above statute reveals that this provision is aimed at punishing conduct. Section 1(6) provides a defence if one became a member before the organisation was proscribed and if one has not taken part in any of its activities while the organisation is proscribed. Thus what is being punished in reality is the act of joining the proscribed organisation or participating in its activities if one had joined at an earlier date.

But where there is no 'conduct' and it was not the defendant's fault that the prohibited state of affairs has come about, liability is contrary to established principle. In the infamous case of *Larsonneur* (1933) the defendant was convicted of being a prohibited alien who was 'found in the United Kingdom'. The fact that she had been deported from the Irish Free State and brought to England in police custody was described as 'circumstances which are perfectly immaterial'. She was 'found here'; the fact that she did not voluntarily come here was irrelevant. This notorious case has recently been defended on the ground that the defendant 'was probably the author of her own misfortune' (Lanham, 1976), in that she was attempting first in England and then in the Irish Free State to contract an arranged 'marriage of convenience'. It was therefore her fault that she was deported back to England. But, if it was forsee-able that she would be deported from the Irish Free State, was it for-seeable that she would be deported back to Britain? Might she not reasonably have expected deportation back to her country of origin, France? Further, preceding fault is not mentioned in the judgment. All the circumstances leading up to her being found in the United Kingdom were simply dismissed as 'perfectly immaterial'.

In *Winzar v. Chief Constable of Kent* (1983) the defendant was brought into hospital on a stretcher. The doctor discovered that Mr Winzar was merely drunk and asked him to leave. When he was later seen slumped in the corridor the police were called. They removed him to the roadway, 'formed the opinion he was drunk', and placed him in their car parked nearby. He was convicted of the offence of being found drunk on the highway, it being immaterial that he had been placed on the highway involuntarily. It is possible to argue here that it must have been Winzar's fault that he was in that situation. The report of the case does not specify how he got to be taken to hospital, but the most likely explanation is that he had been found in some public place, or, perhaps, had summoned medical assistance when he was only drunk and not in need of such attention. However, it can also be argued (though perhaps with less conviction) that Winzar could have been found drunk in his own home by a neigh-bour or friend who summoned the medical assistance, in which case he would not have been at fault as we cannot blame someone for getting drunk in the privacy of his own home. Further, there is no hint at all in the judgment of the court that it was relevant how or why Winzar was brought to hospital; no mention was made of pre-ceding fault.

In *Strowger v. John* (1974) the defendant was convicted of an offence, contrary to section 12 of the Vehicles (Excise) Act 1971, of failing to display a valid excise disc on his car windscreen. The disc had fallen from the windscreen while the defendant was at work. It has been suggested that there was prior fault here as 'the accused could, by careful inspection, have guarded against such an occur-rence' (Leigh, 1982). However, such a claim seems implausible as the court found that 'the licence had become detached without any negligence or default of the defendant'. The defendant was, in effect, held liable in the absence of any voluntary conduct.

From these cases it thus appears that English law is prepared, occasionally, to impose criminal liability in the absence of conduct or preceding fault. This is a deplorable state of affairs. Our sense of justice would be outraged by a law that made it a crime to have measles – a condition one is powerless to prevent. The above cases would not seem that different in principle from such a Draconian approach.

(iii) Vicarious liability. In certain limited circumstances the law is prepared to hold a person criminally responsible even though he did nothing himself, but because he is vicariously responsible for the acts of another. This is not the same as accessorial liability where the defendant must act himself in the sense of, at least, helping or encouraging the principal offender. With vicarious liability the acts of one person are simply attributed to another even though that other might be completely unaware that a crime is being committed. In effect this is, like the cases in the preceding section, punishing people for their status or for being in a particular situation.

Fortunately, this concept, which runs counter to all established notions of individual responsibility, is broadly limited to certain situations in which an employer is held liable for the criminal acts of his employee committed within the scope of the latter's employment. This can occur in one of three ways. First, a statute might expressly provide for vicarious liability. For example, section 163(1) of the Licensing Act 1964 provides: 'a person shall not . . . either himself *or by his servant or agent* . . .' do certain things. Secondly, the courts can interpret words in a statute so that the act of an employee is deemed to be the act of his employer. Take for example the word 'sell'. Section 2 of the Food and Drugs Act 1955 makes it a criminal offence to 'sell' improper food. 'Sell' is a legal term referring to a legal contract of sale. Under such a contract, the sale is by the owner of the goods (owner of the shop, store, company or whatever) to the customer. So if a store assistant delivers improper food to a customer, the employer is deemed to have sold the goods (*Coppen v. Moore* No. 2, 1898). Finally, in relation to licensee cases, the courts have developed the 'doctrine of delegation'. Under the Licensing Acts there are many offences which can only be committed by the holder of a licence (the licensee). If the licensee delegates general responsibility to his staff, their acts (and their *mens rea*) are imputed to the licensee. For example, in *Howker v. Robinson* (1973) a barman in the lounge-bar of licensed premises sold liquor to a boy aged fourteen. It was held that the licensee had delegated responsibility for running the lounge-bar to the barman and, accordingly, the licensee was liable. The acts of the barman were deemed to be the acts of the licensee.

The rationale of vicarious liability is that it is the employer who is responsible for appointing his employee, and he has control and authority over him; he must thus be responsible for ensuring his employee commits no criminal offences within the course of his employment; the threat of criminal liability will prompt him into maintaining careful authority over his employee. If the employer were not criminally liable he could simply delegate responsibility to others and acquire immunity from prosecution by avoiding personal knowledge of the commission of offences on his premises.

These arguments hardly seem sufficiently convincing to justify the imposition of criminal liability upon a person who has done nothing, other than be an employer. Clearly, the licensing and other similar legislation needs amending to ensure that employees can themselves be personally liable. If the employer encourages, instructs or helps his employee to commit criminal offences, he can be held responsible under the rules of accessorial liability. But in the absence of such encouragement etc., which does at least constitute some conduct, criminal liability is unwarranted in such cases.

(c) OMISSIONS

The conduct requirement of most offences is generally satisfied by proof of positive action. But in certain circumstances a passive failure to act may constitute the requisite conduct. Some crimes are specifically defined so as to involve criminal liability for failing to act: for example, failing to provide for a child in one's care or failing to file one's income tax return. But for other crimes a mere failure to act will not constitute the requisite 'conduct' unless there is a legal duty to act. Thus a stranger can sit on a park bench and watch a small child drown in a shallow pool; he will incur no criminal liability even though he could have rescued the child with ease. But the father of the child would not be able to refrain from action with the same impunity. He would be under a duty to rescue his child in such circumstances. Breaching such a duty would constitute the requisite 'act' of the crime of homicide (either murder or manslaughter, depending on his *mens rea*).

English law, rooted in the tradition of individualism, has been loath to 'enforce unselfishness' (*Columbia Law Review*, 1952) and compel people to act. The fact that there is a clear moral obligation on the stranger to rescue the child is insufficient. One is only under a duty to act when one is under a legal obligation. Apart from cases where one is under a statutory obligation to act (as in the earlier examples), the law only imposes a legal duty to act where a defendant has assumed, or is in a position of responsibility whereby others reasonably expect that he will act (or would do so if appraised of the facts). There are four main situations where such a common law duty to act has been held to exist.

First, where a *special relationship* exists between the parties; each becomes under a duty towards the other. For example, parents are under a duty to aid their children; husbands and wives are under a duty to aid each other. The basis of this duty might be that the blood or marriage relationship is so strong as to generate a legal duty to preserve life (*People v. Beardsley*, 1907), but the better rationale is that the interdependence that springs from shared family life or close communal living creates a reasonable expectation of assistance which generates the duty to act (Fletcher, 1978). Thus one would generally be under a duty to aid one's lover and probably even a flat-mate (depending on the relationships), but not one's separated spouse or emancipated son or daughter (*Shepherd*, 1862) (although, again, the situation or relationship might be such that there was still a duty to act).

Secondly, where one person *voluntarily assumes a responsibility* towards another whereby that other reasonably expects assistance if necessary, a legal duty to act will have been created. The cases here have mainly concerned defendants who have assumed responsibility for elderly or infirm persons by taking them into their homes (*Instan*, 1893; *Stone and Dobinson*, 1977), but the principle would apply in other cases as well. For example, if two persons engage in a dangerous joint enterprise such as mountaineering, their relationship of mutual reliance would generate a duty to act (LaFave and Scott, 1972).

Thirdly, a duty to assist others may arise out of contract (*Pittwood*, 1902). A lifeguard employed at a swimming pool is obliged to rescue swimmers in trouble. Because of his contract of employment, the swimmers reasonably expect assistance from him.

And finally, where the defendant has created a dangerous situation he becomes under a duty to minimise the harmful consequences flowing from that dangerous situation. In *Miller* (1983) the defendant, while squatting in someone else's house, fell asleep on a mattress without having extinguished his cigarette. He awoke later to discover the mattress was smouldering. He did nothing about the fire, but simply moved to another room and went to sleep again. The house caught fire and the defendant was charged with arson, contrary to sections 1(1) and (3) of the Criminal Damage Act 1971. As he only had *mens rea* at the time he saw the fire and did nothing, the *actus reus* had to be established *at that time*. It was held that as the defendant had himself started the fire he was under a duty to take whatever steps were within his power to counteract the danger he had created – either putting the fire out himself or calling for the fire brigade. Such an approach is consistent with the general principle relating to the assumption of responsibility outlined earlier. Even when our actions are unintentional, they are nevertheless *our* actions and we bear a responsibility for them. Where others are placed in danger from these actions, they expect us to 'do something'. There is an expectation of reasonable assistance which can generate a duty to act.

So in the above limited situations the law is prepared to hold people criminally responsible for their failures to act. How can this be reconciled with the fundamental principle that the law is only concerned with punishing conduct, voluntary human *action*?

A leading criminal philosopher, Gross (1979), has argued that liability for omissions is not an exception to the general requirement that there must be conduct. Using the earlier example of the child drowning in a shallow pool, he would argue that the requisite conduct is the sitting on the park bench without rescuing the child. The sitting on the park bench is the conduct, but it is only criminal when done in circumstances where someone to whom one owes a duty is in need of rescue. Many legitimate activities (for example, driving) become criminal when performed in an unacceptable manner (for example, recklessly). While the stress in omissions 'is on what must be done additionally if there is not to be liability' (in the main example, rescuing the child), 'liability nevertheless is *for doing* certain things without doing certain other things' (sitting on the park bench without rescuing the child). Gross uses the example of failing to file an income tax return. The *conduct* that is being punished here is *residence in the state* without filing a return.

The more usual explanation, however, is that passivity is just as much 'willed conduct' as is activity. 'Conscious non-motion is a greater assertion of personality than casual acting' (Fletcher, 1978). The man on the park bench is 'acting', albeit negatively. It is a significant act of will to remain motionless in such circumstances.

If it is thus possible to justify liability for omissions as not being inconsistent with the fundamental conduct requirement, why is such liability restricted to those areas where there is a legal duty to act? Why is there no general duty to act? The argument here is that morality surely condemns the stranger who watches the child drowning when he could easily rescue it; such a man has effectively killed that child. The law ought to reflect such a morality. Further, if one of the objects of the criminal law and punishment is to stimulate socially approved conduct then the imposition of criminal liability in such cases would encourage people to act.

If a general duty to act were introduced, it could operate in one of two ways. It could exist as a separate offence carrying a minor penalty as in many Continental Criminal Codes. The state of Vermont in the United States has such an offence, punishable by a maximum fine of $100 (12 Vermont Statutes, section 519). Thus our stranger on the park bench would not be convicted of murder or manslaughter but of the new special offence of failing to rescue. Alternatively, a general duty to act could replace the existing categories of legal duty, breach of which would constitute the requisite 'conduct' for more serious offences. Our stranger's failure to act would thus, like the father's failure, result in a conviction for murder or manslaughter, depending on his *mens rea*. This more radical approach is unlikely ever to be adopted because, in addition to the objections to creating a general duty to act, canvassed below, there would be special problems here in relation to causation and *mens rea*. It could be difficult to argue that the stranger causes (*in law*) the death of the child whereas the father, by failing to exercise his special responsibility for his child, does substantially cause (*in law*) the death of the child (Clarkson and Keating, 1984). Similarly, it has been argued that the stranger cannot have the requisite *mens rea*. He might, at most, *want* the child to drown, but wanting something to happen is not the same thing as intending it to happen. However, such a view is not totally convincing. One can intend anything over which one has control. One cannot intend that it will be sunny tomorrow – but the stranger can intend the death of the child because it was within his power and control to prevent that death.

The arguments against the introduction of a general duty to act have been regarded by English law as overwhelming. The central argument relates to individual liberty and the view that the law should not encroach upon people's privacy and liberty by forcing them to act. The picture painted is that of a man taking a quiet Sunday morning walk through the park and being called upon to rescue one hapless victim after another! Other objections are of a more pragmatic nature. If a hundred people stood on a beach watching someone drown, would all one hundred be liable and be prosecuted? How much help would need to be given? After dragging the drowning man from the sea, would one be under a duty to provide mouth-to-mouth resuscitation and then drive him to the nearest hospital if necessary? How much danger would the rescuer be expected to risk? What if the rescuer's efforts exacerbated the situation and worsened the plight of the imperilled person?

Many of these objections could be easily countered. If there were a general duty to act, it would be limited by a criterion of reasonableness: the rescuer would only be expected to do what was reasonable in the circumstances. And with regard to the individual liberty argument, it must be remembered that our interests in doing as we like are continually being countered by opposing, greater interests.

55

And which is the greater interest: one's right to sit on a park bench minding one's own business, or the right of the child to life?

Perhaps the law's reluctance to impose criminal liability for omissions is based upon an intuitive feeling that it is simply not as 'bad' to 'let die' as 'to kill'. It is morally wrong, but not *as* wrong, to watch the child drown as to hold its head under the water. On this basis it might be desirable for omissions to be punished to a *lesser extent* when they constitute the requisite 'conduct' for criminal offences. Open acceptance of such a view could also help pave the way to the introduction of a new special offence – 'failing to rescue' – which would not carry a severe penalty, but whose very existence on the statute book would have the symbolic value of underwriting the importance that ought to be attached to the value of human life and bodily safety – even of strangers.

C. BLAMEWORTHINESS

I THE RULE

1. Rationale

We have already seen that generally criminal liability is only imposed upon a *blameworthy* actor whose conduct has caused a forbidden harm (see earlier, page 26). It is not enough that a defendant has simply done the forbidden act or caused the prohibited harm. He must have done so in circumstances in which he can properly be blamed for his conduct. Without such blame or fault he is regarded as 'innocent' – and a civilised society is offended at the notion of punishing the innocent. Further, punishment of the blameless would probably be an ineffective deterrent: the law cannot hope to deter innocent actions, and those who are blameless are in no need of help or rehabilitation; and their very 'innocence' indicates that they present no threat to others and thus society has no need to protect itself from such persons. In short, not only would it be unjust, but also there would be little purpose served in punishing the blameless.

2. Indicators of Blame

We saw in Chapter 1 how man is viewed today as a moral agent and not simply as an instrument of causing harm (page 15). He is regarded as *responsible* for his actions. Being a responsible agent means that man is capable of reason; he is capable of understanding the social and legal norms to which he is subject; he possesses free will. He can thus control his actions and can choose whether to comply with the law or not. (The law thus firmly rejects a school of thought advocating *determinism*. According to this view man is not a free agent always in control of his actions and choosing how to act; instead, his actions are seen as 'determined' by preceding events and conditions.)

It follows that because man is this responsible agent exercising control and choice over his actions, we are able to judge those actions. We can evaluate and discriminate between different actions and attribute praise or blame to the actor – in a manner that would be quite inappropriate if dealing with a non-responsible agent. In an artificial sense one might praise or blame a baby for being good or not, or praise or blame a dog for being quiet or not – but we do not hold the baby or the dog *responsible* for their actions in any meaningful way because their actions are not the product of reason, control and choice. We can judge the *result* (and disapprove of the noise made by the baby or the dog), but not the *agent* because of its non-responsibility.

This notion of responsibility and view of man as a moral agent led to wide acceptance of the view that blame and punishment were only justified if a person had *chosen* to commit a crime. If I deliberately throw my glass on the floor breaking it, you can blame me for my actions because you can disapprove of my choice to act in that way. But if I, acting in a normal, careful manner, were to slip on a loose carpet and drop my glass and break it, blame would be inappropriate; I was not in complete control of my actions and did not choose to break the glass.

This process of choosing to break the law is, of course, a mental process. Such persons are said to have a morally blameworthy *state of mind* – or, in legal shorthand, *mens rea*. Where a person acts with *mens rea* he is a responsible agent who has chosen to break the rules; he is thus blameworthy and deserves punishment. Or to put it another way: the presence of *mens rea* indicates that the defendant is blameworthy. There are other indicators of blame but before exploring them we should examine this main indicator of blame, *mens rea*, in more detail.

(a) MENS REA

Mens rea is the mental element required by the definition of a particular crime. As seen in the preceding section, it clearly embraces those who have made a decision and chosen to break the law. However, *mens rea* is not limited to such states of mind. It also covers those who act realising there is a chance (perhaps only a small chance) of their conduct causing the prohibited result. And in some cases it could even extend to persons who do not anticipate causing any harm, but who really ought to have realised the risks involved in their actions. In short, *mens rea* does not refer to any single state of mind. There are degrees of *mens rea*, most notably intention and recklessness. (Some commentators would describe negligence as a third 'degree' of *mens rea*. However, as negligence refers to a failure to consider risks and thus refers to the *absence of a state of mind*, it will be treated as a separate indicator of blame; see pages 68–73.)

Many crimes may be committed if the defendant has any class of *mens rea*. For example, section 1(1) of the Criminal Damage Act 1971 provides that the offence of criminal damage may be committed either intentionally or recklessly. With such crimes it is, of course, unnecessary to distinguish intention from recklessness; either species of *mens rea* will suffice. But certain other crimes are more limited in their *mens rea* requirements. For example, section 18 of the Offences Against the Person Act 1861 provides that for the offence of wounding or causing grievous bodily harm the defendant must act 'with intent to cause grievous bodily harm'. A similar provision is to be found in the Criminal Attempts Act 1981, section 1(1): one can only attempt to commit a crime if one intends to commit the offence (even if the actual offence itself can be committed recklessly). For these latter crimes it is thus essential to define intention with some precision in order to distinguish it from recklessness.

(i) Intention. A person clearly intends a result when he wants it to happen – when it is his aim or objective. This is so even if the chances of the result occuring are slim: if the defendant shoots at his

victim half a mile away knowing he could easily miss, he still intends to kill his victim if that is what he is trying to do.

But what of a defendant who does not want or mean to cause a result but who realises it will almost certainly occur? The classic example here is the man who plants a bomb in an aircraft to explode in flight; his object is to obtain insurance money; he knows passengers are virtually certain to be killed but he hopes that through a miracle they will avoid death. Does he *intend* the death of the passengers? And what of a defendant who again does not mean to cause a result but who realises that it is a likely or highly probable result of his actions? For instance, he might be playing a variation of Russian roulette with four out of five chambers of his revolver loaded; he points the gun at his victim and pulls the trigger – knowing there is an 80 per cent chance of the victim being killed. Does he *intend* to kill?

For several decades intense controversy has raged through English law concerning the meaning of intention and whether it covers these two situations. In *Hyam* (1975) Mrs Hyam poured petrol through the letterbox of the house of her lover's new mistress in the hope of frightening her into leaving the neighbourhood; she ignited the petrol knowing people were asleep in the house. When two children died in the fire and Mrs Hyam was charged with murder the jury were directed that the necessary intention for murder was established if they were satisfied that Mrs Hyam foresaw death or grievous bodily harm as a highly probable result of her actions. It was not necessary to prove that she wanted that result or that she had aimed at that consequence. The House of Lords upheld this direction, arguably endorsing the view that the word 'intention' did bear such a broad meaning throughout the criminal law.

Such an approach was plainly unacceptable. It involved attributing a highly artificial and unnatural meaning to an everyday concept – something best avoided, especially in the criminal law where most issues of guilt are ultimately decided by ordinary lay persons, namely, the jury or lay magistrates. Further, assigning such a broad meaning to the word 'intention' made it impossible to distinguish intention from recklessness. If a consequence was foreseen as highly probable, this was intention; if it was foreseen as merely probable or possible, this was recklessness! The imposition of criminal liability clearly should not be dependent upon such fine and impracticable distinctions. And, finally, such a broad meaning of intention was morally confusing. Most commentators felt that there was a significant moral difference between wanting a result to occur and merely foreseeing its occurrence as highly probable (Glanville Williams, 1983). While the actor in both situations is in control and is willing to produce the particular evil consequence, his actions become more reprehensible if they are deliberate and purposeful. A man's objectives or aims clearly influence our perceptions of his character as a moral agent. Apart from the fact that the harm is more likely to occur when the actor is trying to produce it, it is this deliberate flouting of the legal order that makes us blame him more than someone who does not mean to achieve the consequence but foresees it as a likely by-product of his actions. Accordingly, many commentators felt that the word and concept 'intention' should be reserved for those actors who actually tried to produce the forbidden consequence – such cases could then be marked out as more serious offences where the defendant would deserve greater punishment.

Responding to these criticisms the House of Lords has now retreated from the position adopted in *Hyam* (1975). In *Moloney* (1985) the House of Lords held that in most cases judges should refrain from elaborating or paraphrasing the meaning of intention; it should simply be left to the jury's good sense to determine whether the defendant acted with the necessary intent. This approach was endorsed by the House of Lords in *Hancock* (1986). Whether a defendant intended a result was a question of *fact* which only the jury, by concentrating on the particular facts before it, could resolve. While it is thus impossible to know what intention means in the criminal law, we can guess that many juries will opt for the common-sense definition, namely, 'as "a decision to bring about a certain consequence" or as the "aim" ' (*Mohan*, 1976). To underline this view, Lord Bridge, delivering the leading judgement in *Moloney* (1985), held that foresight of a consequence as probable, highly probable or likely was *not* the equivalent of, or an alternative to, intention. Juries might *infer* from such foresight that the defendant possessed the necessary intention but they would not be bound to draw such an inference; ultimately, the meaning of intention was completely a matter for them.

In *Moloney* (1985) Lord Bridge added an important qualification. In 'rare' and 'exceptional' cases it might be necessary to give guidance to the jury as to how, and in what manner, they could draw inferences from the facts to determine whether the defendant had the necessary intention. This would occur in those cases where the defendant had a purpose other than causing the prohibited harm – but where that result was an inevitable or likely consequence. For instance, Mrs Hyam's purpose was to terrorise her lover's mistress into leaving town; death or serious injury was a very likely by-product of her actions; guidance or elaboration to the jury would be necessary. The same would be true of both *Moloney* (1985) and *Hancock* (1986) (the facts of these two cases are recited on pages 134–5). In *Hancock* (1986) Lord Scarman recognised that such cases are not at all 'rare' and 'exceptional', and accordingly guidance to the jury will be necessary in most cases where the defendant has a primary aim in acting other than causing the prohibited harm.

Lord Bridge in *Moloney* (1985) laid down guidelines to be employed in such cases: the jury should consider whether the relevant forbidden result was a 'natural consequence' of the defendant's actions, *and* whether the defendant foresaw it as being a natural consequence of his actions. If so, then it would be proper for the jury to draw an inference from this that the defendant intended the forbidden consequence.

These guidelines were disapproved in *Hancock* (1986) because they failed to refer to the *probability* of the consequence occurring which 'may be vitally important'. The greater the probability of a consequence occurring, the more likely that it was so foreseen and, if so, the more likely that it was intended. But, even in such cases, it must be emphasised that this degree of probability of the result occurring was only one factor to be considered by the jury with all the other evidence in determining whether the defendant intended a result.

These decisions, sadly, leave the law in a state of great confusion and uncertainty and open the door to inconsistency in jury verdicts:

possessed with identical facts, one jury might conclude that Mrs Hyam intended death or grievous bodily harm while another jury could reach the opposite conclusion. It is, however, not uncommon to leave crucial issues such as this to the jury. In theft, for instance, the issue of 'dishonesty' is largely left to jury determination (see pages 153–5). However, a concept such as 'dishonesty' involves value judgments; ethical stances have to be taken – and the jury, as the mouthpiece of community values, is probably the most appropriate body to express such judgments. But the same is not true of intention, which involves a consideration of less far-ranging factors than those involved in the concept of dishonesty. In the interests of certainty and predictability it is surely for *the law* to determine what intention means – and in laying down that definition community values should be reflected.

The House of Lords, by leaving intention undefined, is trying to retain maximum flexibility so that juries do not have to resort to perverse verdicts to convict those felt deserving of conviction. Many violent protesters or terrorist bombers who do not necessarily *mean* to kill, for example, could escape liability for murder if a clear and narrow definition of intention were laid down. But now, juries have a free hand to convict where they feel it to be appropriate. They can expand or contract their definition of intention to meet the justice of the particular case.

This is an intolerable position inviting prejudice, discrimination and abuse. It involves the abandoning of all standards in an area of law where it is crucial that standards be clearly laid down. The principle of legality insists that people be clearly informed in advance about what is acceptable or unacceptable conduct. In an effort to lay down a clearer standard, the Court of Appeal in *Nedrick* (1986) has already been forced to attempt a 'crystallisation' of these decisions by holding that a defendant would need to foresee death or serious bodily harm as a 'virtual certainty – barring some unforeseen intervention'. Where a defendant realised that the consequence was 'for all practical purposes inevitable', the inference that he intended that result 'might be irresistible'. While this is clearly a step in the right direction it is nevertheless time for Parliament to intervene to put a stop to this sad judicial saga. Of course, it will be difficult to produce a test of intention acceptable to all, but one test, favoured by many commentators and very similar to the *Nedrick* (1986) test, is the Law Commission's proposal in the Draft Criminal Code that a person acts 'intentionally' in respect of an element of an offence 'when he wants it to exist or occur, is aware that it exists or is almost certain that it exists or will exist or occur' (Law Commission, 1985, cl. 22(a)). Such a test does at least lay down a standard. A diligent jury will know what it is working towards. Inferences, based on probabilities and so on, will still need to be drawn. But they will be inferences towards a clearly specified goal, rather than the present position where applying the *Moloney* (1985) and *Hancock* (1986) guidelines the jury is forced to draw inferences from all the evidence to try and establish something that is totally undefined.

One final point needs mention here. Intention must be subjectively ascertained. It is not a matter of what the defendant ought to have intended. The jury must somehow get into the mind of the defendant and find out what he actually did intend (Criminal Justice Act 1967, section 8). Such a task is of course impossible: we do not have 'intention meters' to plug into a person's brain. So what the jury has to do is draw inferences from the facts; they must consider all the circumstantial evidence – the conduct of the defendant before, during and after the crime, his motives etc. – and from all this infer what he must have intended. The result is that unless the defendant is markedly different from an ordinary person (say, because he is suffering from schizophrenia) the jury will tend to conclude that if an ordinary person would have intended a certain result from his actions, then the defendant must also have had a similar intention. This is, in effect, an 'objective test' of intention: the defendant is deemed to have intended that which a reasonable person would have intended in the circumstances. Nevertheless, while this might be so in practice, it is important that section 8 of the Criminal Justice Act 1967 endorses a subjective test of intention. It ensures that the exceptional defendant (say, one suffering from some abnormality) will be treated on an individualised basis. The question will be: what did *he* intend? It will not be: what would some hypothetical, normal defendant have intended?

(ii) Recklessness. The law has long regarded the reckless wrongdoer as blameworthy and deserving of punishment – but the law has not always been (and still is not) consistent as to the meaning of recklessness.

After a somewhat uncertain and vacillating history, the law appeared to have settled down by the late 1970s to approve a subjective meaning of the concept of recklessness. Under such a test recklessness involved the conscious running of an unjustifiable risk (*Cunningham*, 1957; *Stephenson*, 1979). The defendant must himself have foreseen the possibility or chance of the consequence occurring, and the risk taken must have been one that was unjustifiable or unreasonable to take in the circumstances.

For instance, in *Stephenson* (1979) the defendant crept into a hollow in the side of a large straw stack to sleep. Feeling cold, he lit a fire of twigs and straw inside the hollow! Not surprisingly, the stack caught fire and was damaged. Now, while most people would clearly recognise the risks involved in such an activity, Stephenson was able to establish that he suffered from schizophrenia which could have prevented him foreseeing or appreciating the risk of damage from his act of lighting the fire. Accordingly, he had not been reckless.

Such a subjective test of recklessness is clearly reconcilable with the theory of responsibility outlined earlier (pages 56–7), explaining why we blame people for their actions. A subjectively reckless actor is responsible for his actions. He is in control of his actions and, knowing the possible consequences, has chosen to take unjustifiable risks. We can plainly disapprove of such a choice and blame him for his conduct. We can also hope that punishment will deter him and others from taking similar risks on subsequent occasions. Following this reasoning, we do not blame Stephenson for his actions. Because he was unable to realise what the possible consequences of his actions would be, he did not choose to risk causing harm; to him there was no risk. Accordingly, he was not fully responsible for the consequences of his actions.

But what if Stephenson had not suffered from schizophrenia but had simply not bothered to think about the risks involved in his activities? He might simply have been extremely tired, depressed, drunk or just foolish. Must we still respond: he was not aware of the risks; he did not choose to risk causing harm; he is blameless? Consider, for instance, the archetypal 'fool': the defendant in *Lamb* (1967). Lamb had a revolver with a five-chambered cylinder which rotated clockwise each time the trigger was pulled. The revolver had two bullets in the chambers but neither bullet was in the chamber opposite the barrel. Lamb pointed the revolver at his best friend in jest and pulled the trigger without meaning to do any harm. Unfortunately for all concerned, but most particularly the friend, the pulling of the trigger rotated the cylinder and so placed a bullet opposite the barrel so that it was struck by the firing pin. The bullet was discharged, killing Lamb's friend. Again, must we simply respond: Lamb did not recognise the risks, he thought that as neither bullet was opposite the barrel no harm could possibly result; he thus made no choice to risk causing harm and is blameless? Must we agree with Glanville Williams (1981) that 'Lamb was a fool, but there is no need to punish fools to that degree. There is no need to punish Lamb at all'?

These questions were emphatically answered in the negative by the House of Lords in *Caldwell* (1982) and in *Lawrence* (1982) when Lord Diplock, delivering the leading judgement in both cases, ruled that a defendant was reckless if he:

1. did an act which created an obvious risk of the consequence occurring – an obvious and serious risk according to *Lawrence*, 1982, and
2. when he did the act he either gave no thought to the possibility of there being any risk, or recognised that there was some risk involved but nonetheless went on to do the act.

This constitutes an important extension to the law of recklessness. No longer is liability dependent upon a defendant subjectively recognising the risks involved in his actions; a defendant who has completely failed to consider such risks, such as the defendants in *Stephenson* (1979) and *Lamb* (1967), can now be adjudged reckless (unless it could be argued that Lamb, in particular, had considered the risk, but ruled it out as not possible, thereby failing to come within the new test of recklessness as he *had* given thought to the possibility of there being a risk [Glanville Williams, 1982]). For instance, in *Elliott v. C* (1983) a fourteen-year-old girl who was in a remedial class at school and who had not slept for an entire night poured white spirit on the floor of a garden shed and then threw two lighted matches on the spirit; the shed was destroyed by fire. It was established that because of her age, lack of understanding and experience, and exhaustion, she did not recognise the risk of destroying the shed; even if she had thought about the matter, she would not have realised the risks. However, it was held that the risk was an 'obvious' one – obvious to a 'reasonably prudent person'. Accordingly, she was reckless in not giving any thought to such an obvious risk.

This major swing towards objectivity in the criminal law has been ferociously attacked by commentators (for example, Glanville Williams, 1981; Smith, 1981). And despite the fact that the House of Lords has held that this new test of recklessness is applicable throughout the criminal law (*Seymour*, 1983) the lower courts, including the Court of Appeal, have shown their hostility to the new test by clinging to the old subjective test of recklessness in a few particular areas (*Satnam and Kewal*, 1984: a special subjective test of recklessness for the crime of rape has been supplied by the Sexual Offences (Amendment) Act 1976, section 1(2); *W v. Dolbey*, 1983: the word 'maliciously' in Offences against the Person Act 1861, section 20, which had been interpreted to mean 'recklessly' is unaffected by *Caldwell/Lawrence*, 1982).

The case against objective liability in the criminal law as exemplified by the *Caldwell* (1982) and *Lawrence* (1982) test of recklessness is simple. Responsibility is based upon choice; the defendant must choose to do harm (which includes *consciously* running the risk of causing harm); the defendant who simply fails to think or consider possibilities has not exercised such a choice; he is thus not blameworthy and does not deserve punishment. It is also argued that punishment is pointless under a deterrent theory of criminal law because the notion of deterrence presupposes that defendants have thought about the consequences of their actions; one who is unaware of the risks involved in his actions will hardly be deterred from so acting.

On the other hand, it is possible to support this shift towards objectivity in the criminal law. The fundamental question is whether we blame persons who fail to consider obvious risks and simply go ahead and act. Lord Diplock compared such a state of mind with that of a man who has foreseen the risks of his actions and concluded: 'Neither state of mind seems to me to be less blameworthy than the other' (*Caldwell*, 1982). We do surely blame persons who fail to consider the consequences of their actions. It is this failure to bring to bear one's faculties to perceive risks that is blameworthy. We all have a responsibility to avoid creating obvious and unjustified risks to the safety of others – it is the failure to exercise this responsibility that is blameworthy. If a worker on a high building simply threw bricks down to a crowded street below, injuring pedestrians, we would surely not be impressed by his plea: 'I just didn't think; my mind was elsewhere.' Our response would be: 'You ought to have thought; we blame you for not thinking.' A failure to consider the possible consequences of one's actions expresses a certain attitude towards those consequences: it demonstrates a lack of concern about them. Duff (1980) gives the example of the bridegroom who forgets his wedding – this could only be because he regarded the whole event as quite unimportant. We are surely entitled to blame people when their lack of concern poses risks to the safety of others.

However, such an argument is only plausible *if the actor had the capacity to do otherwise*. We can blame Lamb because he was capable of recognising the risks involved in his actions and ought therefore not to have fired his revolver. But we surely cannot hold responsible and blame the schizophrenic in *Stephenson* (1979) or the young backward girl in *Elliott v. C* (1983). They were not capable of foreseeing the consequences of their actions and therefore could not have assumed the responsibility we expect most people to shoulder; their actions did not demonstrate lack of concern – they were simply the inevitable product of their inadequacy. We can sometimes blame people for their inadequacies if it was their fault they were in such an inadequate condition (for example, if they had voluntarily consumed drugs or too much alcohol) – but no civilised society can blame people for inadequacies over which they have no control – and therefore they ought not to be blamed for the consequences of actions that are purely the result of such an inadequate condition.

So, provided the defendant was capable of appreciating the risks involved in his actions, it follows that there ought to be little objection to blaming and punishing those who simply fail to think. Indeed, there are further considerations supporting punishment in such cases. The subjective theory of criminal liability (which endorses the old notion of subjective recklessness) assumes that the state of a person's mind is ascertainable – that somehow it is possible to establish what was in his mind when he committed the crime, possibly months or even years previously. While this same problem exists with regard to proof of intention, it is even more acute here. Lord Diplock described the distinction between consciously running a risk and failing to appreciate a risk as an impracticable distinction when the only person who knows what was in the defendant's mind is the defendant himself – and even he probably cannot recall accurately. He stated that he was simply not prepared to perpetuate such 'fine and impracticable distinctions' (*Caldwell*, 1982).

And, finally, it is possible to support punishment in such cases on utilitarian grounds. The punishment of a defendant who fails to consider obvious risks might encourage him or others in the future to be more careful. It can prompt persons to take care before acting, to use their mental faculties and to draw upon their experiences so as to anticipate the consequences of those actions. We shall delay exploring the validity of such claims until later when the whole deterrent basis of the criminal law will be subjected to closer scrutiny.

(b) NEGLIGENCE

A person is negligent if his conduct fails to conform to the standard expected of an ordinary reasonable man in his situation, i.e., if on a purely objective basis he fails to exercise the degree of care, skill or foresight that such a reasonable man would exercise.

Negligence is often classed as a species of *mens rea* on the basis that it is a state of mind: it is the failure to think about the consequences of one's actions. Not thinking refers to a state of mind, albeit a blank state of mind. However, such a view cannot be accepted for three reasons. First, it is semantic nonsense to describe a blank state of mind as a state of mind. Presumably, then, unconsciousness would need to be described as a state of mind! Second, a person can be negligent even if he does anticipate the consequences of his actions (i.e. does not have a blank state of mind). Such a person would also be at least reckless – but that does not alter the fact that if his standard of conduct fell below that of the reasonable man he is negligent. Finally, English law has long recognised two degrees of negligence. There is simple negligence which is the same standard as that employed by the civil law and there is gross negligence which involves a major departure from the standards of the reasonable man. If negligence were an empty mind, how could there be degrees of emptiness and negligence? Accordingly, it is better to regard negligence not as part of *mens rea* but as a separate factor indicating blameworthiness.

As seen in the preceding section, the prevailing view until recently was that criminal liability ought generally to be based upon subjective *mens rea*. Thus it was widely felt that punishment for negligence was generally inappropriate. Accordingly, negligence has not been a common basis for the imposition of criminal liability in English law. Simple negligence has been restricted to certain lesser statutory offences such as driving without due care and attention contrary to section 3 of the Road Traffic Act 1972. And even the more serious species of negligence, gross negligence, has only been rarely employed as an indicator of blame: it has been confined to one serious offence – manslaughter.

However, while this still remains the formal position, the reality is more complex, due to two developments. First, over recent years the number of crimes that are in effect crimes of negligence has grown as a result of an increasing trend to convert crimes of strict liability (crimes where no blame need be established – see pages 92–9) into crimes of negligence by providing a 'due diligence' defence. Although the crime is still in theory one of strict liability, if the defendant can show he was not negligent he will be acquitted.

Secondly, the debate over the role of negligence as an indicator of blame sufficient to warrant the imposition of criminal liability in fact continues unabated – but under the guise of new nomenclature, namely, recklessness. The House of Lords in *Caldwell* (1982) and

Lawrence (1982) in laying down a new extended meaning of reck-lessness encompassing a failure to consider risks has, arguably, col-lapsed the erstwhile distinction between recklessness and negligence and made negligence a common basis for the attribution of blame (but under the name 'recklessness'). Indeed, all the arguments canvassed for and against the new recklessness test (see pages 66–8) are simply arguments for and against negligence as an indicator of blame.

There is, however, a *technical* distinction between the two con-cepts. Lord Diplock in *Lawrence* (1982) (but not in *Caldwell*, 1982) actually distinguished recklessness from negligence. Recklessness involved the running of an 'obvious *and serious* risk' whereas simple negligence merely referred to the running of an obvious risk. Further, recklessness necessitated a finding of 'moral turpitude' which was not necessary for negligence. Unfortunately, neither of these terms was defined. Clearly, to Lord Diplock, recklessness was 'worse' than neg-ligence. The best view, it is submitted, is that he was trying to equate recklessness with gross negligence (*Seymour*, 1983).

One further distinction between the two concepts exists in theory. We saw earlier (page 65) that if a defendant considers the possibility that a risk may occur but rules out that risk as not being possible, he will escape the rigours of the *Caldwell* (1982) and *Lawrence* (1982) test of recklessness. But if a reasonable man in his situation would not have so ruled out the risks he would nevertheless be negligent.

Such distinctions are, however, extremely fine and of dubious practical utility. The overlap between recklessness and negligence is substantial even if not complete. The House of Lords in *Caldwell* (1982) and *Lawrence* (1982) can be fairly criticised for blurring these two concepts and depriving us of the vocabulary to distinguish them. But these two decisions have succeeded in one thing. They have pushed to the fore the central issue: should criminal liability be based on objective factors (whether called recklessness, gross negligence or even simple negligence) or is blame and responsibility to be limited to those who possess subjective *mens rea*?

This same debate has for the last century, and particularly over the last decade, been conducted in a slightly different setting, namely, in relation to the law of mistake.

(i) Mistake. For most crimes the defendant must have *mens rea* in relation to the *actus reus*. This means he must have *mens rea* in relation to each of the elements of the *actus reus* (the so-called definitional elements). For instance, the *actus reus* of rape is committed when a man has:

(i) sexual intercourse (i.e. vaginal intercourse) with a woman;
(ii) without her consent.

To be convicted of rape a defendant must have *mens rea* (either intention or recklessness) in relation to both these definitional elements. But problems occur if he makes a genuine mistake, for example:

(i) he thinks he is having anal intercourse (buggery) with a woman;
or (ii) he thinks the woman is consenting.

If responsibility and criminal liability were based purely upon subjective *mens rea*, such a defendant ought to be acquitted – no matter how unreasonable his mistake. However, until recently the law was not prepared to adopt such a stance. Ever since *Tolson* (1889) the law insisted that a mistake had to be reasonable if the defendant was to escape liability. If the mistake was not based on reasonable grounds the defendant would be held liable. This was in fact making negligence the basis of criminal liability. A defendant who made such an unreasonable mistake lacked subjective *mens rea*, but was negligent and was being punished for that negligence.

However, in the last decade there has been a sharp swing away from such an approach and an insistence on subjective *mens rea*. This movement was heralded by the famous House of Lords decision in *Morgan* (1976). In this case a husband invited a number of companions home to have sexual intercourse with his wife. He suggested to them that if she struggled they were not to take it seriously as that was her way of increasing her sexual satisfaction. The men all had intercourse without the wife's consent. At their trial for rape they claimed that because of the husband's story they had honestly believed she was consenting. The trial judge directed the jury in accordance with the then established law that the men would only

71

escape liability if their belief that the woman was consenting was based on reasonable grounds. The House of Lords held that this direction was wrong. If the men honestly believed that the woman was consenting they lacked *mens rea*. The reasonableness or otherwise of their belief was irrelevant – thus, in effect, ousting negligence as a basis for the construction of criminal liability. (It ought perhaps to be pointed out that while the House of Lords held that the trial judge's direction in law was incorrect, it nevertheless dismissed the appeal by applying the proviso to section 2(1) of the Criminal Appeal Act 1968 – that is, a properly directed jury would have dismissed the defendants' story as a 'pack of lies' and would clearly have convicted.)

Another clear illustration of this shift away from basing liability on negligence is to be found in the Court of Appeal decision of *Williams (Gladstone)* (1984). The defendant saw a man dragging a youth along a street and striking him. Leaping to the rescue of the youth, he punched the man who sustained injuries to his face. Had the facts been as he believed them to be he would clearly have escaped liability on the basis that he was acting in 'self-defence' of the youth (see later pages 76–81). However, he had made a mistake. The man, who had seen the youth seize a woman's handbag, was in the process of lawfully restraining him with a view to taking him to a police station. Under the old law the defendant would have escaped liability only if his mistake had been a reasonable one (*Albert v. Lavin*, 1982). However, following the approach endorsed in *Morgan* (1976), it was held that the unreasonableness of the belief was irrelevant because that would involve convicting the defendant on the basis of his negligence. The crime with which the defendant had been charged (Offences against the Person Act 1861, section 47 – see later, pages 119–20) required proof of the following definitional elements:

(i) that the defendant committed an act
(ii) which was unlawful, and
(iii) that resulted in the application of force to the victim.

For criminal liability, *mens rea* had to exist in relation to all three elements. Because of his mistake the defendant thought he was acting *lawfully*. He thus lacked *mens rea* and so escaped criminal liability.

Contrasting these cases with the new recklessness cases of *Caldwell* (1982) and *Lawrence* (1982) and their progeny reveals again the major issue confronting criminal law today: how much do we blame the defendant who did not realise he was causing harm but who ought to have so realised? Do we blame him enough to justify punishing him? The two lines of authority are technically reconcilable: the defendants in *Morgan* (1982) and *Williams (Gladstone)* (1984) could well be said to have considered the risks involved in their actions but to have ruled them out – thus not coming within the net of *Caldwell* (1982) and *Lawrence* (1982) recklessness. However, in spirit, the two sets of cases could not be more diametrically opposed, with *Caldwell* (1982) and *Lawrence* (1982) holding responsible and blameworthy those who *ought* to have considered risks – and *Morgan* (1976) exempting from responsibility and blame all who did not subjectively realise they were doing wrong. It is unlikely that such tensions within the law will be easily settled – but if the criminal law is ever to develop in a coherent manner, central conflicts such as these will need resolution.

(c) LACK OF DEFENCE

We have seen in the preceding sections that, irrespective of the role of negligence or objective recklessness, the law does blame persons with subjective *mens rea*. But even this is not an invariable rule. A person might have intended to cause a harm but we would not blame him if he, say, punched another in the face in order to save his own life. In other words, viewing the matter negatively: we do not blame a defendant if he has a valid excuse or justification for his actions (or, perhaps in certain situations, we might blame him less). These excuses and justifications are termed 'defences'. Most defences in English law are 'general defences': they are complete defences to any criminal charge. Others, however, are partial and/or particularised defences: for example, provocation is a defence only to the crime of murder but does not result in a complete exemption from liability – liability is reduced from murder to manslaughter.

What is the difference between a justificatory and an excusatory defence? When conduct is justified it is, in effect, 'approved' of – or at least tolerated as acceptable conduct. Any harm caused by the defendant is outweighed by the fact that he has thereby avoided an even greater harm or has furthered some greater societal interest (Robinson, 1982). For instance, a defendant acting reasonably in self-defence or a police officer using reasonable force to effect an arrest will have a justificatory defence for his conduct. He has done no wrong. Each is promoting a greater interest, namely, restricting unprovoked aggression, and ensuring the law is enforced, respectively.

Because justified conduct is acceptable conduct, it follows that there is no need to try and prevent such conduct recurring. Not only is the defendant blameless, but also a deterrent or incapacitative sentence would be quite inappropriate. Further, one is entitled to assist a defendant in his justified conduct. He is 'behaving correctly'; one is always permitted to assist others in such behaviour, and, for the same reason, one is not entitled to use force to resist such justified conduct (subject to what has been said above concerning unreasonable mistakes – see earlier, pages 71–2). So, for example, one cannot use force to resist a lawful arrest as this would involve an undermining of the greater interest being protected, namely, the enforcement of the law.

With excuses the focus is on the *actor* rather than the conduct. With an excusatory defence, the conduct of the defendant remains unacceptable or wrong, but because of some excusing condition or characteristic of the defendant, we hold him not responsible (or not fully responsible) for the wrong act. His excuse renders him blameless (or less blameworthy) and therefore it would be unjust to punish him at all (or to the full extent for the crime committed). Thus we do not blame someone for being insane or for being only eight years old; such a person has an excuse for his actions. But because those actions remain 'wrong' and disapproved of, society might feel it necessary to protect itself from repetition of such conduct. Thus despite the insane person being 'blameless', society might wish to commit him to a secure mental hospital, and although the eight-year-old is not 'blamed' for the harm he causes, society may choose to retain some control over him by the institution of civil 'care proceedings'. And, finally, because conduct remains 'wrong' in the case of excuses, it follows that one may not assist such an excused defendant as this would be helping to perpetrate an evil and, similarly, one *can* use force to resist an excused attack. If an insane defendant attacks one, reasonable force is permitted to resist such aggression. The insane defendant is committing a 'wrong' act – and one is always permitted to counter such unacceptable conduct.

(i) Justification. In what circumstances is conduct justified on the basis that it avoids a greater harm or promotes a greater societal interest? Two examples of a justificatory defence were given above, namely, self-defence and public authority (for example, the use of reasonable force by the police in effecting a lawful arrest). Two other such defences can be added to the list. (Necessity and superior orders, defences that are justificatory in nature, will not be discussed here as it is somewhat doubtful whether either exists as such in English law.) First, there is the defence of discipline. Parents are justified in using reasonable force against their children; this power is delegated to schoolteachers while the children are in their care. While this defence could be regarded as opening the door to child-battery (some parents will not always be able to control their violence to moderate levels), the rationale is that the discipline is promoting the superior interest of the welfare of the child; it is in the child's and society's best interests that misbehaviour by children be punished and prevented. Whether this is a sufficient 'superior interest' to justify adults inflicting violence upon children is a highly controversial matter.

Secondly, there is the defence of consent. In certain circumstances the victim's consent is a defence to a criminal charge. Thus if you consent to my cutting open the skin on your toe in order to remove a thorn, my conduct becomes justified, acceptable conduct. The greater interest here is the value of human autonomy. Individuals are free and responsible agents and respect must be given to their right to consent to harms being committed against them. However, in certain circumstances the interests of society prevail over any value attached to human autonomy and consequently consent may not be given to certain types of harm. For instance, one cannot consent to one's own death – euthanasia is not morally acceptable in our society. Nor can one consent to sado-masochistic beatings inflicting injury, such conduct again being morally objectionable. Whether such moralism should prevail over human autonomy is a matter to be considered later when exploring the function of the criminal law (see pages 167–77).

In order to obtain some insight into the workings of justificatory defences, one further defence will be examined – namely, self-defence.

(1) *Self-defence*. The phrase 'self-defence' is misleading as the defence covers not only protection of oneself, but also acts done in defence of one's property and in defence of others. We all have a right to resist threats to ourselves or any interests with which we are closely identified, including proprietary interests which can be regarded as 'interests of personality' (Kadish, 1976). However, the title 'self-defence' is retained here – because of its wide acceptance in common parlance.

In December 1984 Bernhard Goetz was riding on the New York subway when he was suddenly surrounded by four black youths. One of them demanded five dollars. Goetz, who had been mugged some three years previously and had become somewhat obsessed with that incident, drew a .38 pistol and shot the four men he thought were about to rob him. Two of the youths were shot in the back. One of the youths was shot a second time as he lay slumped in a seat. Three of the youths were carrying screwdrivers, but this fact was unknown to Goetz. After the shooting Goetz fled. All four youths were seriously injured; one was paralysed from the waist down. Despite being initially hailed as a hero, the 'subway vigilante' Goetz was eventually charged with attempted murder, assault, reckless endangerment of other passengers in the subway and with unlawful possession of a firearm. If this case were heard in the English courts, would Goetz be able to plead successfully that his actions were justified on grounds of self-defence?

'Vigilantism is private enterprise in the justice business' (Will, 1985). It is clearly the function of the law to preserve law and order and protect the innocent. While people might have reservoirs of rage waiting to burst out and might fantasise about killing and humiliating those who threaten or offend them, the reality is that we do not live in the Wild West or in a Charles Bronson movie – but in a so-called civilised society. And in such a society it is imperative that the right of the individual to self-help be restricted. Nevertheless, there must be circumstances when self-help is necessary – when it would be impracticable or unrealistic to rely upon the arrival of official help. But for this self-help to be justified, it must be *necessary*. If it was necessary for Bernhard Goetz to do all he did in order to protect himself, then his actions were justified and he is free from blame. But if the force used was not necessary to repel the attack – if he was a vigilante taking the law into his own hands or a disturbed individual striking back in hatred or vengeance – then his actions cease to be justifiable and we can blame him for his excessive response.

A determination of whether the defensive force used was necessary involves a consideration of four issues. With each of these one is ultimately balancing the competing interests of the initial aggressor and the defender – but as the aggressor was the culpable one responsible for starting the violence, the law has tended to tip the scales in favour of the defender. This bias in favour of the defender goes a long way towards explaining how these issues have been resolved.

First, was *any* defensive action necessary? The four youths might never have posed any physical threat to Goetz at all. Had he declined their request for five dollars they might have done nothing. On the other hand, irrespective of what might actually have occurred, Goetz was scared; to him the threat was real and he believed he was about to be mugged. Until recently, English law has insisted that the defender's belief that defensive action was necessary must have been reasonable. Only if a reasonable man in Goetz's situation would also have believed he was about to be physically attacked would defensive action be permitted. Such an approach is surely correct. If the reasonable man would have made the same mistake there can be no question of our blaming Goetz (in relation to this first issue). The law ought to recognise, and indeed praise, those who act in a reasonable manner.

However, as we saw earlier in relation to the law of mistake (pages 71–3), the recent trend here, as exemplified by *Williams (Gladstone)* (1984), has been away from the objective standard of reasonableness. The idea is that if the defendant genuinely believes that defensive action is necessary then he is not blameworthy and must be judged according to his belief. This means that if Goetz were paranoid or neurotic and believed he was about to be attacked when, say, a youth on the subway had merely asked him the time, we would have to judge his conduct as though he were actually about to be attacked. In balancing the interests of aggressor and defender this seems to be excessively biased in favour of the defender – especially as there is no actual aggressor in the example! As was argued earlier, the objective requirement of reasonableness is there to isolate the blameless from the blameworthy. The fact that someone has acted unreasonably, or has made an unreasonable mistake, is one of the indicators of blame and ought not to be swept aside in such a manner.

The second important issue is whether one is under a duty to retreat if possible when faced with aggressive force. Goetz, for instance, did not try and escape although he could probably have retreated to the other end of the subway car, where some twenty other passengers were gathered. Would this failure to retreat mean that defensive force was unnecessary? There is a conflict here between two opposing views. The first view insists that one should be allowed to hold one's ground and not be forced by an aggressor to the 'ignominy, dishonour, and disgrace of a cowardly retreat' (Beale, 1903). The opposing view is that in a civilised society, while cowardice might be regrettable, it is infinitely worse to resort to violence that could possibly be averted. The English courts have, perhaps understandably, tried to steer a middle path between these two extremes and have held that while a person is not under a positive duty always to retreat, the defender ought to demonstrate that he does not wish to fight. His failure to retreat will be one of the factors to be taken into account in determining whether the defensive action was reasonable and necessary *(Julien*, 1969; *McInnes*, 1971). On this basis, if the Goetz case were being heard in an English court, the failure to retreat would certainly indicate that defensive force was unnecessary, but it would by no means be conclusive of that fact.

The third issue concerns the immediacy of the threatened violence. It is often stated that the anticipated attack must be imminent and that one is not justified in using force to repel violence that will only occur in the future. But the courts, again desirous of providing extra consideration to the defender as opposed to the aggressor, have held that anticipatory self-defence can be justifiable in certain circumstances. In *Attorney-General's Reference (No. 2 of 1983)* the defendant's shop had been damaged and looted during the 1981 rioting in Toxteth. Fearing further attacks, he manufactured ten petrol bombs to protect himself and his shop. These expected attacks never materialised. The defendant was charged with possessing an explosive substance contrary to section 4 of the Explosive Substances Act 1883. However, the Court of Appeal ruled that his actions were justified on grounds of self-defence. He was possessing the bombs for a 'lawful object' (self-defence) and therefore could not be liable as section 4 exempts those who act with a 'lawful object' from liability. If one was allowed to defend oneself in the face of an attack, one must be allowed to prepare oneself for such defensive force. The defendant was not confined for his remedy to calling the police or boarding up his premises.

The implications of this decision are potentially alarming. One of the charges brought against Bernhard Goetz was unlawful possession of a firearm. Presumably, following the reasoning in *Attorney-General's Reference (No. 2 of 1983)*, arming oneself for one's own protection against a genuinely anticipated attack is a justifiable act. Goetz, because of his previous mugging and because of widely held views as to the dangerousness of New York subways, would probably be able to establish such a genuine fear and could therefore escape liability on this count. The implications of such an approach hardly need spelling out. Clearly some anticipatory defensive action must be permitted, but not as much as the *Attorney-General's Reference (No. 2 of 1983)* could allow. Perhaps the better approach would be simply to insist that the threatened force must be reasonably imminent. Possibly, an exception could permit the carrying of an offensive weapon in public for self-defence if there was 'an imminent *particular* threat affecting the particular circumstances in which the weapon was carried' (*Evans v. Hughes*, 1972). At the time of taking his gun into the subway Goetz was not fearing a reasonably imminent attack; there had been no particular threat to him.

Accordingly, his plea of self-defence on this count ought to fail.

The final issue relating to self-defence concerns the proportionality of the defensive response. The general rule is that the response must be proportionate to the attack; the defender may only use such force as is reasonable in the circumstances to repel the attack. Assuming some defensive force from Goetz was necessary, the issue becomes whether he could have averted the danger with lesser force – say, with a push or a punch or even by threatening the youths with his gun without firing it. Was it reasonably necessary for him actually to fire the gun?

Again, however, in balancing the interests of defender and aggressor the scales have become heavily weighted in favour of the defender. In *Shannon* (1980) the Court of Appeal ruled that if the defendant thought that what he was doing was necessary, that was 'most potent evidence' that only reasonable defensive action had been taken. In a crisis a defendant could not be expected to weigh up precisely the measure of his necessary defensive action. This seems to suggest that as long as the defender is truly acting in self-defence (as opposed to responding in angry retaliation or pure aggression), the degree of force used is immaterial. Indeed, in the earlier Privy Council decision of *Palmer* (1971) it was stated that the defence of self-defence would only fail if what the defendant did was not done by way of self-defence.

Despite this trend away from the requirement of proportionality, it is doubtful in reality whether the English courts will completely abandon the requirement that the degree of defensive force must be reasonable in the circumstances. Indeed, two closely related and overlapping statutory provisions (Criminal Law Act 1967, section 3; Police and Criminal Evidence Act 1984, section 117) both specify that only 'reasonable force' may be used (in the prevention of crime, and by a police constable exercising his powers, respectively). It would surely be unthinkable that the English courts could endorse the view that simply because Bernhard Goetz thought it was necessary to fire five bullets into youths who demanded five dollars that that meant he had only responded proportionately to his aggressors.

A final point deserves mention. If a plea of self-defence succeeds, the defendant's actions are justified and he escapes liability. If the plea fails, he is fully liable for the crime charged. One possibility, which has not yet been adopted by English law, is that where the defendant was acting to defend himself but the defence fails – say, because he used too much defensive force – then, although his actions are not justified, he has an excuse or a partial excuse. Particularly in the context of homicide, the doctrine of partial excuse could be most useful here: the defendant's liability could be reduced from murder to manslaughter. The Australian courts have long adopted such an approach to excessive self-defence (*McKay*, 1957; *Howe*, 1958). After all, the defendant whose defence fails (because, say, the response was excessive) is blameworthy – otherwise his defence would have succeeded. But, because he was acting to protect himself, he is less blameworthy than another who acted coldly and deliberately. A lesser level of criminal liability and less punishment is therefore appropriate.

(ii) Excuses. In what circumstances is conduct excused on the basis that because of some excusing condition or characteristic of the defendant we exempt him from full responsibility and blame for the wrongful act? We have already seen in introducing the concept of excuses that insanity and lack of age are classic examples thereof (pages 74–5). Similar in nature is the defence of automatism (pages 40–6). With all three of these defences it is the abnormal condition of the defendant that is the basis for excusing his conduct.

The defence of duress is usually thought to be excusatory in nature and is well established in the United States as such. This defence operates when a defendant is threatened with serious violence if he does not commit a crime. He thus commits the crime to avoid the evil to himself. Such conduct is not justified: it is not 'right' or acceptable conduct – the defendant ought not to have the power to choose to harm an innocent person rather than be harmed himself. Nevertheless, such a person is not responsible for his actions. We saw earlier (page 57) that the notion of responsibility involves being able to *choose* to commit a crime or not. A person who has been subjected to overwhelming threats is unable to make such a free choice. He has been deprived of a 'fair opportunity' (Hart, 1968) to choose to obey the law. His actions are 'morally involuntary' (Fletcher, 1978). Accordingly, he is excused from blame. English law has, however, placed strict limits upon the circumstances in which such a person is so excused. For instance, the defence is not available for the crime of murder (*Howe*, 1987) and for other crimes is only available when the defendant is faced with threats of death or really serious injury.

The essence of an excusatory defence is that because of some excusing condition or characteristic the defendant is relieved of responsibility and blame for his wrongful act. However, the excusing condition need not be such as to provide full relief from responsibility. It might simply be a *partial excuse* which results in a reduction of blame but not complete exculpation. Blame is not an absolute 'all or nothing' concept. There are degrees of blame. We will generally blame the intentional wrongdoer more than the negligent one. So, too, we might blame certain actors less because they have some excuse for their actions (but not a sufficient excuse to render them blameless).

Provocation is a good example of a partial excuse. It is a partial excuse to murder only, reducing the defendant's liability to manslaughter. (Other crimes do not have fixed penalties and therefore provocation can be taken into account as a mitigating factor at the sentencing stage.) The essence of provocation is that the defendant must have been so provoked as to lose his self-control and that provocation must have been sufficient to make a reasonable man in the defendant's situation do as he did (Homicide Act 1957, section 3, as interpreted by *DPP v. Camplin*, 1978). For instance, in *DPP v. Camplin* (1978) the defendant, a fifteen-year-old boy, was forcibly buggered by a man. When the man started to laugh and gloat over his sexual triumph, the defendant lost his self-control and beat the man to death with a nearby chapati pan. The House of Lords held that this could amount to provocation because the defendant had clearly been so angry as to have lost his self-control – and a reasonable boy of that age who had just been buggered might well have responded in a similar way.

The focus in provocation is on the defendant's loss of self-control which makes him less blameworthy; it recognises man's inability always to be able to control his emotions. But this 'temporary failure of his inhibitory resources' (Gross, 1979) is not a complete excuse. The law sets a high standard, demanding self-control of all persons. If the defendant cannot meet that standard he must be held liable to some degree – but clearly to a lesser degree than if he had killed in cold blood or out of sheer malevolence.

The whole premise upon which the law of provocation is based is highly suspect. If the defendant lost his self-control but no reasonable person would have done likewise, then it is perfectly legitimate to blame the defendant for failing to act as a reasonable man would have acted. But if a reasonable man in the defendant's situation would also have killed, blame of any degree seems inappropriate. The law can set a standard to try and make people behave as reasonable men would. If a person conforms to this standard, it seems absurd to convict him of manslaughter. On this basis it is suggested that provocation should operate sometimes as a partial excuse (if a reasonable man would not have been so provoked), and at other times as a complete excuse (where a reasonable man would have responded in a similar manner).

Two other partial excuses exist in English law: diminished responsibility and intoxication. Diminished responsibility, like provocation, is a partial excuse to murder only, reducing liability to manslaughter. The excusing characteristic of the defendant is that he must have suffered from 'such abnormality of mind . . . as substantially impaired his mental responsibility for his acts' (Homicide Act 1957, section 2). Such a defendant is still partially responsible for his actions – but to the extent that he is partially irresponsible he is afforded a partial excuse which, if successful, enables the judge to avoid the mandatory sentence of life imprisonment for murder and impose a lesser sentence instead.

It is appropriate now to consider in more detail two important excusatory defences: insanity (a complete excuse) and intoxication (usually a partial excuse).

(1) *Insanity*. Responsibility connotes full control over one's actions and a power to choose whether or not to abide by the law. An insane defendant lacks such full control and power of choice. Accordingly, he is not responsible for his conduct and is excused from criminal liability.

Lack of control and the ability to make effective choices can be caused by external factors, internal factors or a combination of the two. Where the cause is external, such as a blow on the head causing concussion, the law is content to exempt the defendant fully from responsibility and allow his acquittal on grounds of automatism (see earlier, page 40). If the cause is external but is the defendant's fault, such as consuming hallucinogenic drugs, the law will hold the defendant responsible and blame him for consuming the drugs. On the other hand, where the lack of control and ability to choose has an internal, or partly internal, pathological cause, the law is torn in two directions: on the one hand, it recognises that it would be unjust to punish such a person who is sick rather than wicked but, on the other hand, this very illness could cause him to act in the same way again; he is thus regarded as potentially dangerous and in need of restraint. Accordingly, where a person is found to be insane the result is the 'special verdict' of not guilty by reason of insanity. The judge *must* then order the defendant to be admitted to a 'special' secure hospital specified by the Home Secretary. The defendant will be detained there for as long as the Home Secretary directs – possibly for the remainder of his life.

The legal test for establishing insanity was laid down in 1843 by the McNaghten Rules which require that the defendant, at the time of committing the act, must have been 'labouring under such defect of reason, from disease of the mind, as not to know the nature and quality of the act he was doing; or if he did know it, that he did not know what he was doing was wrong'.

This test is so narrow as to be virtually useless. In effect, it only covers those defendants who, in extreme states of mental illness, are unaware of what they are doing or of the significance of their actions. Classic examples here are: throwing a baby on a fire thinking it is a log of wood; cutting off someone's head thinking it will be great fun to see him searching for it when he wakes up – and so on. But most of such defendants would be so mentally ill as to be unfit to stand trial. Where a person is too mentally ill to be able to partici-pate meaningfully in his trial, he can be found unfit to plead and committed to a mental hospital to be released if and when the Home Secretary so directs. The result is that the insanity defence is only employed by those who are 'very mad' but at the time of the trial are no longer manifestly insane.

Further, most defendants who do stand trial are unwilling to plead insanity. Particularly since the abolition of the death penalty, most prefer imprisonment to indefinite detention in a 'special' hospital. If the charge were murder, the defendant might well be convicted of manslaughter only on the basis of diminished responsibility. In such an event, and for all other charges, the defendant might even escape prison by receiving a hospital order under the court's powers contained in the Mental Health Act 1983. As a result, it is perhaps not surprising that in 1982 out of 2023 defendants whose mental disorders were recognised by the court in their trial, only one person actually received a 'special verdict'.

Statistics such as these have led some commentators to urge that the insanity verdict should be abolished. It has become nothing more than 'an ornate rarity, a tribute to our capacity to pretend to a moral position while pursuing profoundly different practices' (Morris, 1982). The gist of the argument is as follows: there are many mentally ill people in our prisons for whom the insanity defence was not available; if mental illness is an excusing condition, the law is being applied in a grossly uneven manner. But, more fundamentally, ought mental illness to be an excusing condition at all? Many people might be mentally ill and commit a crime but there is little evidence to suggest that the one causes the other. The classic position is that the insane are mad and not bad. But why cannot the same person be both mad and bad? At a different level, Morris (1982) argues that while there might be a relationship between mental illness and crime, a stronger relationship exists between adverse social circumstances and criminal behaviour. Being born to a one-parent family living on welfare in a black inner-city area is a stronger pressure towards committing crime than any mental illness. Why is there an insanity defence but no defence of 'social adversity'?

It must be noted that under the civil law insane persons can be committed to hospital against their will. The fact that such a person has committed a crime is irrelevant to such civil commitments. Under these abolitionist proposals, where a person *has* committed a crime he would be criminally prosecuted in the normal way. If he had *mens rea* he would be convicted, and then any mental illness would be taken into account *at the sentencing stage*. His sentence, of course, could not then exceed that available to a sane defendant convicted of the same offence. If, on the other hand, *mens rea* could not be proved – because of mental illness or for whatever other reason – the defendant would have to be acquitted, but, of course, if he were perceived to be dangerous, civil commitment proceedings under the Mental Health legislation could be instituted.

Adopting such a solution, it is argued, would avoid the present confusion of roles and conflict between the disciplines of law and psychiatry. At present psychiatrists have to appear as witnesses in criminal courts and answer legal questions such as: did he know the nature and quality of his act? (An unanswerable question unless the psychiatrist is prepared to distort his testimony to fit the 'manifest absurdity of the McNaghten test' – Royal Commission on Capital Punishment, 1953.) Under the proposed solution lawyers could argue in court about matters they understand – moral choice, guilt and innocence. And at the sentencing stage or in the civil commitment proceedings the psychiatrist could give meaningful testimony in terms of appropriate treatments and so on.

In 1982 Idaho became the first state in the United States to abolish the insanity defence (Idaho Code, section 18–207, Supp. 1983). All issues of insanity were eliminated from the criminal trial; the defendant is either found guilty or not guilty depending on proof of *mens rea* or other matters affecting the elements of the offence charged. Mental illness only becomes relevant at the sentencing stage. It ought perhaps to be mentioned that Idaho's abolition of the insanity defence was not so much in response to the arguments suggested above, but was a result of the mood of anger and public outrage in the United States following the acquittal of John W. Hinckley on the ground of insanity, following his attempt to assassinate President Reagan. Idaho is a very conservative and isolated state; there was a strong belief that the insanity defence was never more than an attempt to 'hoodwink' the jury; it was open to fraud and misrepresentation and usually employed only as a last resort by guilty defendants; it resulted in dangerous defendants being released as 'cured' far sooner than they would have been had they been sentenced on the basis of guilt.

These motivations underlying the Idaho response to the problem seem inapplicable in England where the defence is hardly ever utilised and where detention is usually for far longer than if the defendant had been sent to prison. Indeed, the two most notorious murderers of the last decade, Sutcliffe (the Yorkshire Ripper) and Nilsen (who murdered and then dismembered the bodies of young men in his room), both claimed to be suffering from mental illness, yet neither advanced the insanity defence. But while the defence might not be open to abuse in the same way in this country, what of the earlier arguments for abolition of the insanity defence?

Judge Bazelon stated in one of the most famous United States insanity cases that 'our collective conscience does not allow punishment where it cannot impose blame' (*Durham v. United States*, 1954). And this surely is the central and proper function of the insanity defence as an excuse. We excuse the weak and hold them blameless (or less blameworthy). We excuse a defendant subjected to duress; we recognise the plight of the helpless; it is a concession to human infirmity. So too with insanity. The mentally ill are clearly 'weak'. Our whole culture endorses the view that respect ought to be paid to human autonomy and dignity – and compassion should be shown for the weak. The insane offender is so 'obviously different' from most people that we are prepared to excuse him. Also, the insane offender is immune to the deterrent messages of the law and therefore punishment for individual deterrence is pointless. And even in terms of general deterrence, the main function of conviction and punishment is to stigmatise the *wicked* in order to affirm minimum standards of conduct. The general public is unlikely to identify with an insane offender; he is too different – no lessons can be learnt from his experience.

Accordingly, it is submitted that the insanity defence ought to be retained as an excuse in the law. Of course, the McNaghten Rules are far too narrow and need to cover many more defendants suffering from mental illness. Also the powers of indefinite detention available under the present law need overhauling so that no person found 'not guilty by reason of insanity' can be detained for longer than the maximum sentence available for the crime committed. The McNaghten Rules have been largely abandoned in the United States and serious reforms proposed in this country (Butler Committee, 1975). Discussion of such proposals is beyond the reach of a book of this nature, but the central point remains: in an institution of blame and punishment such as the criminal law, there must be room for excuses when responsibility is lessened. It is not simply that mercy is a part of justice. It is that justice is deeply offended by the punishment of the insane. Accordingly, a substantially reformed insanity defence is a necessary part of the construction of the criminal law.

(2) *Intoxication*. Intoxication can be caused by the consumption of either alcohol or other drugs (or a combination of the two). While the precise effect of each drug on the human central nervous system is different, alcohol and many other drugs have the initial common effect of releasing inhibitions causing some persons to do things they would not normally do. In such cases the actor is still fully aware of what he is doing and, accordingly, the law refuses to recognise such partial intoxication as any form of excuse. The law simply adopts the view that 'a drunken intent is nevertheless an intent' (*Sheehan and Moore*, 1975). Such an approach is inevitable. The actor has not lost all control and the ability to reason; he can still be adjudged responsible for his actions, and to the extent that his abilities are impaired, he can be blamed for such impairment and not excused. On purely practical grounds it would be impossible to allow the consumption of, say, three or four pints of beer to operate as an excuse. The evidential problems posed by such an approach would be insuperable – and, of course, it could actually encourage drug consumption followed by crime.

The real problem faced by the law is not such cases where drink or drugs causes imprudence, but rather the rarer cases where there has been an excessive consumption of alcohol or drugs or where a more powerful hallucinogenic drug such as LSD has been taken. In such cases the drugs can have the effect of impairing ability to foresee consequences. One can become so intoxicated that one loses awareness of what one is doing. For instance, in *Brennan v. HM Advocate* (1977) the defendant consumed between twenty and twenty-five pints of beer, a glass of sherry and a quantity of the drug LSD. He then stabbed his father to death with a knife. In such a state of extreme intoxication, his claim that he was unaware of his actions becomes plausible. And clearly, at the time of stabbing his father, Brennan was not responsible for his actions; he lacked control over his actions; he possessed no ability to reason and make choices. Indeed, all the hallmarks of responsibility were missing.

However, in another sense, Brennan was responsible for the death of his father. He was responsible for getting himself so intoxicated. If drugs had been slipped into his tea without his knowledge, he would obviously bear no responsibility for his subsequent actions. But where the defendant chose voluntarily to consume drink or drugs he can be held responsible for anything that happens while in such a state of voluntary intoxication. In our culture everyone knows the potential consequences of excessive drinking or drug-taking. Everyone can therefore be deemed to know the risks involved and can be blamed for such risk-taking.

Of course, the logical correlative of this is that a person cannot be blamed if he takes a drug that is not generally known to cause such extreme intoxication. Thus in *Hardie* (1984) it was held that Valium and other sedative or soporific drugs must be treated differently from alcohol and other drugs that cause 'unpredictability or aggressiveness' because the effects of Valium and such drugs were not generally known.

But where the effects are generally known, such a casting off of the 'restraints of reason and conscience' (*Majewski*, 1977) is a reckless thing to do. If the crime that the defendant commits is one that can be committed recklessly then his intoxication is no excuse. The requisite *mens rea* of the crime, recklessness, is established by proof that the defendant voluntarily got himself intoxicated (*Majewski*, 1977).

Such an approach, while understandable in the policy terms that the law is not prepared to 'let drunks get away with it', has been severely criticised. Until recently recklessness bore a subjective meaning: the defendant himself had to foresee the possibility of the harm occurring. Most defendants who drank themselves into oblivion would not possess such foresight and therefore could hardly be adjudged reckless in the true sense of the word. It was criticism such as this that induced Lord Diplock to redefine recklessness in objective terms in *Caldwell* (1982). Now it is irrelevant whether the defendant foresaw the risk himself; all that matters is whether the risk would have been 'obvious' to the reasonable man. In *Caldwell* (1982) a drunk defendant set fire to a hotel. He was charged, amongst other things, with the offence of damaging property with intent to endanger life or being reckless whether life would be endangered, contrary to section 1(2) of the Criminal Damage Act 1971. He claimed that he was so drunk at the time that it never occurred to him that the lives of the people in the hotel might be endangered. Applying his new objective test of recklessness, Lord Diplock was able to conclude that the act of setting fire to the hotel did create an obvious risk of endangering life and therefore the defendant was reckless; his lack of subjective foresight was irrelevant.

While the law has generally adopted this approach of blaming the defendant for becoming so intoxicated, there has also been a feeling that in many cases the responsibility of a drunken defendant might be *reduced*. He is less in control of his actions than his sober counterpart. He is also probably less dangerous as his drunkenness will deprive him of any steadfast resolve to commit the crime. In a sense, the position of a drunken defendant who is unaware of his actions at the time of the crime is analogous to that of a negligent wrongdoer – who deserves punishment but not to the same extent as the intentional wrongdoer. Thus while Brennan was clearly to be blamed for becoming so intoxicated and then killing his father, he was not as blameworthy as a sober man who deliberately kills another.

In most cases the law has deemed it to be unnecessary (and in fact, not possible) to allow intoxication to operate as a partial excuse at the substantive level. The reduced level of blameworthiness can be reflected at the sentencing level. Caldwell, for instance, could be found guilty of the substantive offence and then receive a lesser sentence than his sober counterpart would have received. Such an approach has the added advantage of allowing fine-tuning in the sentencing to reflect the actual extent of the drunkenness. But this approach could not be adopted in relation to the crime of murder which carries a fixed penalty (formerly, the death penalty and now life imprisonment). Accordingly, the law developed a rule that intoxication could be a partial excuse to crimes of 'specific intent', of which the most notable example was murder. A drunken defendant would be excused liability for murder but would be convicted of the 'lesser included offence' of manslaughter, a crime of 'basic intent'. He could then receive whatever sentence was felt to be appropriate to reflect his actual degree of blameworthiness. (A lesser included offence is one that contains all the ingredients of the greater offence. When a defendant is charged with the greater offence, for example, murder, a jury can acquit of that offence if unsatisfied that the greater offence elements have been proved – the *mens rea* of murder – but convict of the lesser included offence – manslaughter – if satisfied that the lesser offence elements have been established.)

This approach would have caused no problems if the law had simply stated that murder was in a special position and drunkenness was a partial excuse thereto, reducing liability to manslaughter. But instead, by adopting the broader stance that intoxication was a defence to all crimes of 'specific intention', the law was thrown into confusion. Having developed this absurd and meaningless construct, the law found itself having to define it. What was a crime of 'specific intent'? The judicial tale of attempts to define crimes of specific intent verges at times on the theatre of the absurd (*Beard*, 1920; *Gallagher*, 1963; *Bratty*, 1963; *Majewski*, 1977) and cannot be recounted here. Suffice it to conclude that the cumulative effect of these cases and *Caldwell* (1982) is as follows:

Drunkenness is only a defence to crimes of 'specific intent'. These are crimes that can *only* be committed *intentionally, and* in which the *mens rea* extends beyond the *actus reus*. The defendant must intend to do something more than that which is specified in the *actus reus*. Take, for instance, assault with intent to resist arrest, contrary to section 38 of the Offences against the Person Act 1861. The *actus reus* of this offence is the same as that of a common assault, namely, causing one's victim to apprehend immediate physical force. The defendant must have *mens rea* in relation to this but *in addition* he must also intend to resist arrest. This additional element of intention makes this offence one of 'specific intent'. It will have the practical effect of reducing liability to the 'lesser included offence' of common assault, an offence of 'basic intent' to which drunkenness is no defence.

The illogicality of such an approach is manifest. The whole concept of 'specific intent' was devised to enable drunkenness to operate as a substantive *mitigating* factor to certain crimes, particularly murder. But, as a result of the above definition, drunkenness is sometimes a partial excuse (where there is a lesser included offence of basic intent) but sometimes a *complete defence* – as with theft where no lesser included offence exists. There is no rationale underlying such a distinction; the result is sheer chance. Also, applying this definition strictly, it is difficult to see how murder itself can actually be classified as a crime of specific intention. While it is true that since *Moloney* (1985) murder is a crime that can only be committed intentionally (a proposition that was probably not true under the pre-1985 law of *Hyam*, 1975), it nevertheless remains difficult to see how the *mens rea* of murder can be said to extend beyond the *actus reus* (see pages 135–8). It does seem somewhat ironic that the definition of 'specific intent' does not fit the very crime it was designed to accommodate!

The law is clearly in a state of confusion – largely because of a judicial reluctance to articulate openly the aims of the law in this respect. It is submitted that the true policy of the law here is (and should be) that we blame the drunken defendant for causing a harm, but we blame him less than his sober counterpart. Drunkenness is thus truly a partial excuse. The defendant is less responsible and deserves less criminal liability – for all offences. If drunkenness cannot be utilised as a *substantive* mitigating factor (and it cannot as not all crimes have their lesser included counterparts) then it should be relegated to being a mitigating factor in sentencing. If this latter course were adopted, special provision would need to be made for murder to ensure that drunken defendants escape the mandatory sentence.

II. THE EXCEPTION – STRICT LIABILITY

While the general rule insists upon proof of blame as a prerequisite to the imposition of criminal liability, there is an exceptional category of crimes for which no such blame need be established. The defendant can be convicted even though he had no *mens rea* and was not blame-worthy in any other way. These are called crimes of strict liability.

Take for instance the House of Lords case of *Alphacell Ltd v. Woodward* (1972). The defendant company were paper manufacturers whose premises were adjacent to a river. Their manufacturing process produced effluents which were run into filtration equipment designed to prevent the effluents entering the river. The equipment was regularly examined and well maintained. Nevertheless, due to a pump becoming blocked on one occasion, effluent was discharged into the river. Their conviction for causing polluted matter to enter the river contrary to section 2(1)(a) of the Rivers (Prevention of Pollution) Act 1951 was upheld by the House of Lords. The fact that they had not known and had no reason to believe that the pollution was taking place was irrelevant. The offence was one of strict liability.

The development of most strict liability offences dates from the nineteenth century. In the aftermath of the industrial revolution a great deal of regulatory legislation was enacted dealing with the new areas of public health, safety and welfare. The trend increased in the twentieth century as an increasingly complex society demanded social regulation. Legislation dealing with traffic regulation, consumer protection, control of impure food and drugs, protection of the environment and so on was steadily passed.

Much of this developing regulation could have been placed under administrative control without involving the criminal law. For instance, local authorities could have been given powers to close down or in some other way to restrict the operations of companies causing polluted matter to enter rivers. But instead of adopting such an approach, it was felt that the criminal law would be the most effective instrument for enforcing such regulations. Invocation of the criminal sanction would best stimulate the required diligence and cause persons engaged in such activities to police their enterprises to ensure compliance with the law. Also, of course, many of these activities do cause real and serious harms: causing polluted matter to enter rivers clearly harms the environment. The criminal law has always been one of the traditional mechanisms of social control and prevention of harms.

But, accepting such a view for the moment, why were the traditional principles of the criminal law not incorporated into such regulatory offences? Why was the requirement of blame or fault dispensed with? The true reason relates to problems of law enforcement. Proof of blame could have undermined the efficacy of the law. Take, for instance, offences relating to the sale of impure or adulterated food or drugs. Advances in chemical analysis meant that adulteration became easier to detect but the huge increase in the standard of products, and the increased complexity of their component ingredients made it extremely difficult to prove that a manufacturer or merchant knew that the goods did not conform to standards (Leigh, 1982). If *mens rea* needed to be proved, the law would become a dead letter.

While these practical considerations of enforcement were the real reason for the proliferation of strict liability offences, other justifications were soon added. Strict liability would promote increased care and efficiency. Knowledge of strict liability is a cost to be weighed when setting up a trade or business. It will encourage enterprises to appoint experts, say chemists or bacteriologists, to ensure that their products are safe. It is preferable to place the burden on such enterprises who are in a position to prevent the harm than on the innocent public.

Another line of justification is that no injustice is caused as strict liability offences are not 'real crimes'. They are only quasi-criminal offences, 'regulatory violations'. Conviction does not entail the same stigma as for real crimes. The penalties are usually slight. Prosecutorial discretion usually insists upon prosecution only of those who are in some way to blame. In other cases, should the truly blameless be prosecuted and convicted, a minimal sentence such as an absolute discharge would be appropriate.

And, finally, it is argued that the sheer volume of regulatory offences necessitates dispensing with *mens rea* or other indicators of blameworthiness. It would simply be too time-consuming if blameworthiness had to be proved in every case of, say, parking on a double-yellow line.

Despite such claims (the validity of which will be explored shortly), the courts have been cautious about interpreting offences as imposing strict liability. Most crimes of strict liability are statutory and it is for the courts to interpret these statutes to ascertain whether an offence of strict liability has been created. The relevant statutory provision in *Alphacell Ltd v. Woodward* (1972) imposed criminal liability 'if he causes . . . to enter a stream any poisonous, noxious or polluting matter'. No word pointing to *mens rea* or blame was used – but that did *not* necessarily mean the offence was one of strict liability. The provision needed to be interpreted according to established principles of statutory interpretation to ascertain whether Parliament intended the offence to be one of strict liability.

The most important of these principles is the now well-established presumption in favour of *mens rea*. Lord Reid in the leading case of *Sweet v. Parsley* (1970) stressed that there was a clear presumption that Parliament did not intend to make criminals of persons who were in no way blameworthy in what they did. This presumption is particularly strong where the offence is 'truly criminal' in character (*Gammon Ltd v. AG of Hong Kong*, 1984). Where the offence is of a public welfare nature lacking social obloquy – and particularly where it deals with a field of activity in which the public has little choice whether to participate (for example, buying food and drink or breathing the air) – there will be a greater readiness to rebut the presumption in favour of *mens rea*.

But even with regard to these latter offences the presumption can only be rebutted if it seems clear, having examined the relevant provision in its full statutory context, that this is what Parliament intended. Further, the presumption will only be rebutted if it can be shown that the imposition of strict liability will be effective to promote the objects of the statute by encouraging greater vigilance to prevent the activity in question (*Gammon Ltd v. AG of Hong Kong*, 1984). If the creation of a strict liability offence would not help promote observance of the law because, say, the defendant could not have done anything to avoid breaking the law, then there is no point in imposing strict liability (*Lim Chin Aik*, 1963). Finally, it is sometimes asserted that the less severe the penalty, the more likely it is that Parliament intended to impose liability without fault. Such a view, however, must be treated with caution. Certain offences of strict liability carry severe penalties including terms of imprisonment. Lord Scarman pointed out in *Gammon Ltd v. AG of Hong*

Kong (1984) that there is not necessarily anything inconsistent in such an approach especially where the rationale of those offences is their deterrent effect: a severe penalty will be a more significant deterrent.

Despite this judicial emphasis on the presumption of *mens rea* and caution in allowing its displacement, the fact nevertheless remains that there are countless offences of strict liability in English law raising crucial questions. Can one justify the use of strict liability in the criminal law on moral or utilitarian grounds? If not, could the same degree of regulation of the various activities involved be achieved without the invocation of the criminal law, say, by administrative processes?

The justifications of strict liability were considered above. The case against strict liability is a strong one. It is unjust and morally indefensible to punish the blameless. A person who does not know he is doing wrong and who has taken all reasonable precautions to avoid harm (i.e. was not negligent) does not deserve criminal conviction and punishment. Describing such offences as 'quasi-criminal' or 'violations' is no more than a semantic evasion which 'seems rather like saying that it is all right to be unjust so long as you are not too unjust' (Brett, 1963). No matter how trivial, a strict liability offence is still a crime which can result in prosecution and conviction in the criminal courts. Such moral condemnation is unjustifiable in the absence of blame.

Further, it is simply not true to assert that all offences of strict liability are minor offences carrying lesser penalties. In *Hussain* (1981) the defendant was convicted of unlawful possession of a firearm contrary to section 1 of the Firearms Act 1968 even though he believed it was merely a toy used by his son. The court held that this offence, carrying a maximum penalty of three years' imprisonment, was one of strict liability. Such an offence can hardly be described as a 'mere violation'. While supporters of the strict liability doctrine could point to the fact that Hussain was only fined £100 (presumably because of his lack of blameworthiness), it nevertheless remains the case that he was convicted of a criminal offence clearly involving odium and he was made to forfeit a significant sum of money – hardly a 'just' solution.

Finally, in relation to blame, it is often asserted that no injustice occurs in reality, as in most cases prosecutions are only brought against those who are in fact blameworthy. For instance, Viscount Dilhorne, who participated in *Alphacell Ltd v. Woodward* (1972), has declared that in his opinion the company was at fault in installing their filtration system where they did (Leigh, 1982). Such an explanation simply cannot be accepted. A criminal conviction carries with it the moral condemnation of the community; this cannot be made dependent on the private judgment of prosecutors. Further, the assertion cannot be true of all cases. The defendant company in *Alphacell Ltd v. Woodward* (1972) was fined £20 and ordered to pay in all £24 costs – hardly the sort of penalty that would have been imposed had the justices felt it was to blame for polluting the river.

Turning to the utilitarian arguments, there appears to be little evidence that the imposition of strict liability makes people more careful. Some persons involved in the sorts of activities generally regulated by strict liability offences will simply regard any fines incurred (the typical penalty) as a licence fee for operating as they do. Others, if they are to retain their competitiveness in the market, will generally only be able to afford to take such precautions *as are reasonable*. In other words, the imposition of strict liability achieves nothing in deterrent terms that could not be achieved by making all such crimes ones of negligence. Further, a blameless operator does not need rehabilitation or incapacitation (the other two established objectives of the criminal sanction) – or if he did, this could be better achieved by administrative control and sanction (see below, page 98).

What, finally, of the arguments of expediency – that it would be too difficult and time-consuming to have to prove *mens rea* or other blame in each case? Clearly, administrative convenience cannot be allowed to dictate the contours of the criminal law: no one would suggest making theft an offence of strict liability simply because of the vast number of prosecutions that are regularly brought and the difficulty of establishing *mens rea*. Also, it is doubtful whether the existence of strict liability saves that much time and money in many cases as *after conviction* there needs to be some enquiry (albeit not subject to the same burden of proof) as to blameworthiness in order to fix the appropriate sentence. If the defendant company in *Alphacell Ltd. v. Woodward* (1972) had been deliberately dumping effluent in the river, their punishment would have exceeded the £20 fine that was imposed.

Despite the weight of such arguments, it is submitted that it would be naive to contemplate the decriminalisation of all offences of strict liability or their wholesale conversion into offences involving fault. Some minor regulatory crimes, such as parking offences, that are widely perceived as not being 'truly criminal' and that carry a minimal penalty must clearly remain as offences of strict liability. But for the remainder, there are two possible courses of action.

The first alternative is to decriminalise the conduct as such and make it subject to administrative regulation by administrative processes. Such procedures are already extensively used. Factory inspectors, health and safety officers and other such persons regularly inspect premises and often seek improvement by cooperation and persuasion. Other administrative remedies are at their disposal: planning permissions can be revoked or modified, enforcement and stop notices issued and so on. Leigh (1982), for example, cites the enforcement scheme created by the Health and Safety at Work Act 1974 which in 1977 resulted in 6233 improvement notices and 2666 prohibition notices being issued, compared with only 1600 prosecutions being commenced. Such non-criminal alternatives could be far more effective than prosecutions. Faced with the threat of closure of their premises, for example, a business will quickly effect the necessary improvements – and far sooner than if they merely had to pay a fine as the cost of their infraction.

The other alternative is to convert existing offences of strict liability into ones requiring some degree of blame – most probably, negligence. Such an approach has already been adopted in relation to many former strict liability offences by the introduction of 'due diligence' defences. The crime remains prima facie one of strict liability, thus not increasing the prosecutor's burden – but if the defendant can show that he was not negligent, he will escape liability. Thus the crime effectively becomes one of negligence – except in relation to the burden of proof. Canadian and Australian law have developed general due diligence defences applicable to all crimes of strict liability. English law, on the other hand, has preferred a more selective use of such defences with notable examples to be found in such important legislation as the Trade Descriptions Act 1968 and the Misuse of Drugs Act 1971.

Clearly there is room for further expansion along such lines. What is needed is a conscious reappraisal of all strict liability offences with a view to determining which can be decriminalised and made subject to administrative regulation, which need to remain as criminal offences but with due diligence defences added, and, finally, which *minor* offences can remain as pure strict liability offences.

D. CAUSATION

We have seen that for 'result crimes' criminal liability can only be imposed upon a blameworthy actor whose conduct has *caused* the forbidden harm. Without this causative link being established the defendant must escape liability. In *White* (1910) the defendant tried to murder his mother and gave her a drink containing poison. The mother had a taste of the drink and then, quite by chance, had a heart attack and died. White could not be convicted of murder because it was not his conduct that had caused her death (he was, however, convicted of attempted murder).

The problem faced by the law here is one of defining the necessary circumstances for the establishment of causation. When is the causal link between an act and an event established? In what circumstances will it be broken? In *Lewis* (1970) a wife locked herself in her third-floor flat and refused to admit her husband, claiming he had previously inflicted great violence upon her. He shouted threats at her including a threat to kill her and she heard the sound of breaking glass. She was in another room but, terrified of what he might do, she jumped from the window and broke both her legs. It was held that the husband's actions had caused her injuries. They had not been 'self-inflicted'. Is it possible to discern any principle or policy behind such an approach? What would have been the position if instead of throwing herself from the window the wife had committed suicide by shooting herself? Would it have been held that the husband had caused her death?

It is interesting (and instructive) to note how little interest has been paid by English law to the issue of causation. Attention, both judicial and otherwise, had focused primarily on the notion of blameworthiness. The irony is that much of blameworthiness is established by proof of mental elements that are in reality elusive and incapable of precise proof. Causation, on the other hand, need not be linked to mental elements and could be capable of purely objective (and thus realistic) ascertainment. Indeed, it could be argued that the way forward for the criminal law would be to tighten up and clarify the rules on causation which could lead to a diminution of the importance of the doctrine of *mens rea* in particular. However, the law has eschewed such an approach and rarely tried to develop any coherent principles, with the result that 'the entire field of causation in criminal law is utterly bankrupt' (Schulhofer, 1974).

The problem of causation can be approached in several ways. One view is that there are no underlying general principles at all. The courts simply resort to considerations of 'policy' to determine whether a particular defendant has caused a specified harm. Whether or not causation is established is no more than a 'moral reaction' or a 'value-judgment' (Glanville Williams, 1983). While many of the cases appear only to be explicable in terms of such a policy-oriented analysis, such an approach is fraught with problems and opens the door not only to inconsistency in verdicts, but also to inconsistency in prosecutions as prosecutors, too, will only be guided by 'policy' or their 'moral reactions' in deciding whether to prosecute. Also, while 'policy' might explain why a defendant, say Lewis, was prosecuted and convicted of an offence, it is not at all clear that the policy considerations dictate liability for *the* offence charged. Why was Lewis found guilty of inflicting grievous bodily harm? If 'policy' dictates he be liable for a crime, why not for *an assault* – which seems to be what he really did? If his wife had shot herself, would 'policy' dictate he be liable for a homicide offence? Answers to such questions are not possible once one has abandoned principle for an *ad hoc* approach.

Another view is that an analysis of causation cannot proceed independently of the criterion of blameworthiness and, going further, is dependent on it. Causation cannot be judged in purely objective physical terms. It must be assessed in terms of blameworthiness and responsibility. According to this view, if blame can be established, the result cannot be that remote and therefore causation is deemed to be established. If a defendant has, say, *mens rea*, he will usually expect the harm to result. Causation will almost certainly be established where the defendant has reason to expect the result (Gross, 1979).

While such an approach certainly goes some way towards explaining the criminal law's relative lack of interest in causation, it cannot be accepted as a true explanation of the issue of causation. According to this view, once it had been established that Lewis was blameworthy this automatically resolved the problem of causation. But again the question becomes: blameworthy in relation to what crime? Lewis was clearly blameworthy in relation to a common assault but it was only on a somewhat technical basis that he was adjudged to have *mens rea* in relation to inflicting grievous bodily harm (see page 120). And what if Lewis had been insane? Insanity would have relieved him of responsibility and blameworthiness. Must one then conclude that an insane person cannot cause a harm? And, conversely, it is obviously not true that a finding of causation must necessarily flow from a finding of blameworthiness. Let us alter the facts of *Lewis* (1970) and assume that he wanted to kill his wife. He knew she was neurotic and would leap from the window. He expected her to die from the fall. Mrs Lewis did jump but, by chance, landed unhurt. Unfortunately for her she landed at the feet of a sadistic mugger who shot and killed her. In this altered situation Lewis had the *mens rea* of murder; his actions have led to a chain of events that ultimately resulted in the death of his wife. But nobody would seriously suggest that Lewis caused the death of his wife. She was killed by the mugger. Thus all the 'real work' cannot be left to be done by the concept of blame or *mens rea*. Some principles or *rules* on causation *are* necessary and it is to a summary of these principles, crude as they are, that we now turn.

It is generally stated that there are two main principles of causation in English criminal law. First, the defendant's actions must be a 'but for' cause of the result (a *causa sine qua non*). 'But for' Lewis shouting his threats and breaking the window, his wife would not have jumped from the window. This insistence upon factual causation is natural. It would be an intolerable violation of any principle of personal responsibility to hold a person liable for a harm he did not cause at all. But as the altered facts of *Lewis* (1970) above indicate, a 'but for' cause is not sufficient to attribute causal responsibility. 'But for' Lewis's actions, his wife would not have been shot by our hypothetical mugger. His actions were therefore, in a sense, *a* cause of her death – but merely being a 'but for' cause is not enough. A second requirement must be satisfied. The defendant's actions must be the 'operative' or 'proximate' cause of the result. These words mean no more than that the defendant's actions must be the *legal* cause of the prohibited result as well as being the factual cause.

This second requirement of legal causation is satisfied where the defendant's actions are a sufficiently direct cause of the result. One way of determining this is to ask whether some other cause of sufficient significance 'intervened' to break the causal chain. Many events or causes can 'intervene' or contribute towards the ultimate harm. But not all will break the chain of causation. Suppose Lewis had broken into the room and struck his wife. Being thrust backwards by the blow she tripped over a chair and fell out of the open window. This tripping and falling is a contributory or 'intervening' cause of her ultimate injury – but it is a *dependent intervening cause*; its occurrence was dependent on and closely connected to Lewis's blow. Such dependent intervening causes are of insufficient significance to break the causal link. But in our earlier *Lewis* (1970) and the mugger variant, the act of the mugger shooting Mrs Lewis was an *independent intervening cause* (a *novus actus interveniens*); its occurrence was independent of and not immediately connected to Lewis's actions. Such an independent intervening cause will break the causal link and exempt Lewis from responsibility for his wife's death.

These two examples are of course extreme and thus 'easy' ones. The real problem arises when faced with the exact facts of *Lewis*

(1970). Mr Lewis was outside the matrimonial flat. On hearing his threats and the breaking window, Mrs Lewis jumped and sustained injuries from that fall. Her act of jumping was clearly a contributory or 'intervening' cause of her injuries. How does the law determine whether it was a dependent or an independent intervening cause?

While the answer to this question is by no means clear, some broad principles can be extracted from the authorities. The Law Commission in their Draft Criminal Code Bill 1985 (Law Commission, 1985) argue that their proposal represents the present law. Clause 21 (1) provides that 'a person causes a result when . . . his act makes a more than negligible contribution to its occurrence . . . unless . . . some other cause supervenes which is unforeseen, extremely improbable and sufficient in itself to produce the result.'

This is based on the test adopted in *Roberts* (1971) where a girl leapt out of a moving car in order to avoid the sexual advances of the defendant. It was held that if the girl's actions were reasonably foreseeable causation was established. However, if her jumping from the car was 'daft' or 'unexpected', the causal link would be broken. Thus according to this analysis it must have been regarded as reasonably foreseeable that Mrs Lewis would try and escape by jumping from the window. Lewis could be said to have reasonably expected his wife to act in such a manner. On this basis while it might (at most) be reasonably foreseeable that she would try and escape by jumping and injuring herself thereby, it would not be reasonably foreseeable that she would shoot herself. Such an action would be 'unforeseen, extremely improbable and sufficient in itself to produce the result'; Lewis would therefore not be responsible for his wife's death had she shot herself.

Related to this central principle is the commonly stated proposition that a voluntary intervention by a third party will break the causal chain (Hart and Honoré, 1985). The mugger in our earlier *Lewis* (1970) variant was an independent third party acting voluntarily. His actions would break the chain of causation. Another way of stating this same proposition is that it was completely unexpected and unforeseeable that he would be there and would kill Mrs Lewis. This point was raised in *Pagett* (1983). The defendant, holding a girl as hostage and shield, opened fire on police attempting to arrest

103

him. The police officers returned the fire and their bullets hit and killed the girl. It was held that the defendant's acts had caused the death of the girl. The 'intervention' of the police was *in effect* involuntary; they were acting in reasonable self-defence. Goff LJ declared that there was no distinction between a reasonable attempt to escape violence and a reasonable attempt to resist violence by defending oneself. Thus the morally involuntary conduct of the police was reasonably foreseeable; it was a *dependent* intervening cause which did not exempt the defendant from liability.

A final well-established proposition does however pose some problems in reconciliation with the central principle. It is commonly stated that the defendant must take his victim as he finds him. This causes no problem with regard to the physical condition of the victim. If the victim has a thin skull or a weak heart and a single blow from the defendant kills him, causation is clearly established. There is no intervening act even of a dependent nature. An existing condition cannot be regarded as an 'intervening' event. But problems arise when this proposition is extended to psychological conditions or beliefs. In *Blaue* (1975) the defendant stabbed a Jehovah's Witness, piercing her lung. It was established that with a blood transfusion she would have survived. Because of her religious beliefs, however, she refused the transfusion and died. The Court of Appeal expressly rejected the argument that an unreasonable refusal to have a blood transfusion would break the chain of causation. Instead, they ruled that the defendant must take his victim as he finds him and this 'means the whole man, not just the physical man'. Thus it makes no difference whether the victim has a thin skull, a religious belief that forbids him medical attention or is a neurotic liable to leap out of windows for little cause. The defendant must take his victim as he finds him in mind and in body.

With this last principle in mind let us consider a final variant of *Lewis* (1970) and his defenestrating wife. Suppose now that Lewis is a generally non-violent man who lives on the twentieth floor of an apartment-block. He and his wife are having an argument in the course of which he threatens her with minor violence – say, a light slap. Unknown to her husband, Mrs Lewis is in fact neurotic and pathologically terrified of any physical force. She runs into the next room and leaps from the window (or takes out a revolver and shoots herself). Under *Roberts* (1971) such action is plainly 'daft' and 'unexpected' and would constitute an *independent intervening cause*. But under the *Blaue* (1975) qualification Lewis must take his wife as he finds her, neuroses and all; he has caused her injuries.

The best way of reconciling these tensions within the law would be as follows. The central principle of reasonable foresight or expectation as established in *Roberts* (1971) should prevail. However, in ascertaining whether the victim's response was reasonable, account must be taken of particular idiosyncrasies of the victim. Thus, in *Roberts* (1971), the girl was 'normal'. The question is simply whether her response was reasonable. In *Blaue* (1975) the question becomes one of ascertaining whether it was reasonably foreseeable that a Jehovah's Witness would refuse a blood transfusion, and in our final *Lewis* (1970) variant the issue is whether one could reasonably foresee or anticipate that a neurotic wife might act as Mrs Lewis did. This test has the advantage of taking account of the victim's condition but limiting the chain of causation to reasonable responses from such a victim, and it is surely right that we all be held causatively responsible for all the reasonably predictable consequences that flow from our actions – but not responsible for the outlandish or occasionally totally unpredictable consequences that can follow therefrom.

E. THE FORBIDDEN HARM

The final element in the construction of criminal liability is the necessity of establishing that the blameworthy actor's conduct has caused *the forbidden harm*.

The nature of the requisite forbidden harm of course varies from crime to crime. For homicide offences the victim must have been killed; for rape the woman's vagina must have been penetrated by the defendant's penis; for theft the victim must have been deprived of his property or some interest therein – and so on.

1. The Importance of Harm

An obvious question raises itself at this point. Why does the criminal law generally insist upon proof of such direct harm? If an assassin aims his gun and fires at his intended victim, why should it matter whether he kills, wounds or misses the victim? His conduct and degree of blameworthiness are the same whatever the outcome. If his liability, or the extent of his liability, is to depend upon the result, is this not reducing the criminal law to a lottery? Why should chance (whether he hit or missed) be relevant in our moral assessment of his actions? In *Krawec* (1985) the defendant killed an elderly pedestrian by carelessly driving his motorcycle. He was convicted of driving without due care and attention. The Court of Appeal, reviewing his sentence, stressed that the primary consideration was the quality of the driving. The fact that he had happened to kill someone was not relevant. The question for consideration here is whether this approach of disregarding the significance of harm should be adopted throughout the criminal law.

There are several related reasons suggesting that the stance taken in *Krawec* (1985) is ill-conceived. The fact is that we do judge people by the *results* of their actions and not simply on the basis of the quality of their actions and their exertions. If a student makes a spectacular effort to hand in a good essay that is assessed for examination purposes but sadly the resultant product is appalling nonsense, his tutor might, in recognition of his endeavours, treat him sympathetically in private – but the essay must ultimately be judged on its objective merits. He will get an appropriate low mark, reflecting the result and not the quality of his efforts. This is the mark he deserves and in fairness to him (in according him the respect and dignity owed to a responsible human being) and in fairness to his fellow students (who will make comparative judgments in relation to their essays and marks) this is the mark he must receive. And the converse is equally true. If the most idle and cavalier student puts in a minimal effort but fortuitously spots all the relevant points and turns in an excellent essay, he must get an excellent mark. His essay must again be judged by its results and not on the basis of how hard he tried.

This same approach is surely appropriate to the defendant in *Krawec* (1985). Of course we can and must judge the quality of his actions (his careless driving in itself) but the fact that his actions have resulted in the death of a human being totally alters our moral judgment. His actually killing someone arouses resentment in society (quite apart from the bitterness and pain caused to the relatives and friends of the deceased). Imagine ourselves as observers. We see Krawec riding his motorcycle and going through red traffic lights. He does not see an elderly pedestrian but misses him by inches. Our reponse is one of momentary fright: 'Did you see that? How can people drive like that?' we exclaim indignantly, but, thankful no harm occurred, we forget the incident and return to our routines. But if we as observers witness these same events but this time the elderly pedestrian is in Krawec's path and is knocked over and killed, we do *not* simply respond: 'How can people drive like that? And what bad luck that the old man was in his way', as the Court of Appeal in *Krawec* (1985) seems to feel we ought to respond. Our reaction is now one of horror. He has *killed* the pedestrian. His driving was not just dangerous, that is, likely to cause danger. The danger has materialised and someone lies dead. We do not simply forget the incident and return to our lives. The resultant harm makes its mark; it leaves a lasting impression. If Krawec tries to drive away we will chase him or ensure we have his registration number. In short, our entire reaction to the event is profoundly affected by the *results* of the dangerous driving. Such condemnation and resentment is relevant in determining the level of Krawec's criminal liability and punishment, and suggestions to the contrary by the Court of Appeal in that case ignore clear moral distinctions drawn in everyday life.

This approach is reinforced if we view the events from Krawec's or any other defendant's own point of view. Those who cause harm feel greater remorse than those who have 'close calls' (Fletcher, 1978). If we had been driving and had narrowly missed the pedestrian, our prime reaction would be relief – not guilt. But if we had knocked him over we would know that our actions had now had a permanent and concrete impact on the lives of others. Feelings of guilt and remorse are truly appropriate when harm has been caused – again, a natural response that ought to be reflected by the law.

2. Attempts

In many respects the law does accept this premise as to the importance of harm. Our initial assassin who fired his gun would be guilty of a more serious offence (murder) if he killed his victim than if he merely wounded him. But in some respects the law has adopted a more equivocal stance. For instance, if our assassin had missed completely he would nevertheless be liable for attempted murder. Following the central argument, this should presumably be no offence as there is no direct harm, or at least a lesser offence carrying a lesser punishment. Californian law accepts this latter proposition and provides that an attempt carries a penalty of one half of the penalty available for the full offence (California Penal Code, section 664). English law, on the other hand, has endorsed the opposite view and provides that irrespective of the lack of direct harm, attempts to commit crime are punishable to the same extent as the completed offence (Criminal Attempts Act 1981, section 4(1)).

It is submitted that this English approach is unjustifiable. Despite the obvious case that the attempter is just as dangerous, blameworthy and in need of rehabilitation and deterrence as he who successfully completes the crime, the fact remains that no direct harm has resulted from his actions. It is relatively easy to justify the imposition of *some* criminal liability for attempts. In addition to the utilitarian case of equal dangerousness etc., it can be argued that attempts do cause a harm – an indirect or 'second order' harm (Gross, 1979). We all have an interest in being secure from harm. Attempts are dangerous and pose a real threat of harm; that threat violates our security interest and right to autonomy; someone has encroached upon our 'territory' in a menacing manner. Violations of such interests are 'harms'. Nevertheless, they are clearly *lesser* harms than direct or 'first order' harms and ought to be treated as such by the law. And, indeed, it does appear that *in practice* the English courts do accept such reasoning. While section 4(1) permits the same level of punishment for attempters, in reality they tend to receive substantially lesser punishments than are meted out for completed crimes. For instance, in *Foster* (1985) a mother who tried to kill her two children by drugging their Weetabix was put on probation for two years. Had the children died, and had she been convicted of murder, she would have received a sentence of life imprisonment.

3. Attempting the Impossible

A related problem presents itself. Can there be criminal liability for attempting the impossible? If the direct harm cannot possibly be committed, can there be even a 'second order' harm justifying criminal liability? Or are the utilitarian arguments (equal dangerousness etc.) sufficient in themselves to justify the imposition of criminal liability in the absence of any harm?

Consider the two classic examples of attempting the impossible. First, a pickpocket places his hand in the victim's empty pocket. The crime here is physically impossible; there is nothing for him to steal. Can he be liable for attempted theft? Secondly, the defendant handles goods believing they are stolen but, unknown to him, they are not stolen (the facts of *Haughton v. Smith*, 1975). Here (unlike the first example) the defendant has done all that he means to do but what he has done turns out not to be criminal. The crime is legally impossible as the goods are not stolen. Can he be liable for attempting to handle stolen goods?

The common law answered these questions in the negative (*Partington v. Williams*, 1975; *Haughton v. Smith*, 1975). The crime was impossible and so the defendant's acts could never get close enough to *the crime* to satisfy the *actus reus* of attempt; one could not get 'proximate' to nothing! (See earlier, pages 29–30.) A conviction in such cases would be a conviction purely on the basis of guilty intentions. Believing that goods were stolen, for instance, did not make them stolen goods. Accordingly, without the possibility of direct harm occurring, there could be no criminal liability for an attempt. One could support such an approach. If the crime was not possible the defendant's actions posed no social danger; they constituted no threat to the interests of others. There was thus no 'harm' even of a second-order nature.

109

Such arguments were however unacceptable to those who argued that a person who tried to commit a crime is as morally blameworthy and in need of incapacitation and rehabilitation as he who succeeds; punishment is needed to deter him and others from attempting similar crimes again; whether the crime is possible or impossible could be mere 'chance'. It was these arguments that finally won the day and resulted in the enactment of the Criminal Attempts Act 1981, section 1(2) of which provides: 'A person may be guilty of attempting to commit an offence to which this section applies even though the facts are such that the commission of the offence is impossible.'

And section 1(3) confirms the self-evident proposition that where a person believes the facts to be such that he would be committing a crime, he is to be regarded as having the necessary intention to commit the offence. This means that a defendant who intends to handle a particular radio believing it to be stolen when in fact it is not stolen cannot argue that he intended to handle a 'non-stolen radio'. Section 1(3) makes it plain that if he believed the radio was stolen, he intended to handle a 'stolen radio'.

However, the House of Lords in *Anderton v. Ryan* (1985) was not prepared to travel such a subjectivist route and, in a quite extraordinary manner, declared that the statute would lead to 'asinine' results and proceeded to subvert the legislation from its original purpose. In this case Mrs Ryan had bought a video recorder believing it to be stolen. She had confessed as much to the police who were investigating a burglary at her home. However, there was no actual evidence that the video recorder was stolen and so it had to be treated as though it were not. She was charged with dishonestly attempting to handle a stolen video recorder contrary to section 1(1) of the Criminal Attempts Act 1981.

The House of Lords held that there could be no liability on facts such as these, with Lord Bridge (with whom the majority agreed) drawing a distinction (nowhere to be found in the statute itself) between 'acting in a criminal way' and 'objectively innocent acts'. Only if the defendant was acting in a 'criminal way' could there be liability if the commission of the crime turned out to be impossible in the circumstances. For instance, the pickpocket who sticks his hand into another's empty pocket is acting in a 'criminal way' and would be liable. But if the defendant's acts were 'objectively innocent' (as Mrs Ryan's were) there could be no liability. Mrs Ryan had done all she meant to do by handling the goods, but her completed actions did not in law amount to a crime because the goods were not stolen. Section 1(4) limits the law of attempt 'to any offence which, if it were completed, would be triable . . . as an indictable offence'. Mrs Ryan's actions 'were completed' and did not amount to an indictable offence as required by section 1(4). The same would be true of the man who has sexual intercourse with a girl over sixteen believing her to be under that age. His actions are 'innocent'; he has done all that there is for him to do but what he has done is not, in law, an indictable offence. To hold him liable for an attempt would be to convict him purely on the basis of his 'guilty thoughts'. On the other hand, the pickpocket has not completed what he set out to do, but if he had, a criminal offence would have been committed; if he had achieved his objective he would have completed the full indictable offence of theft.

This distinction between 'objectively innocent' acts on the one hand and 'criminal' or 'guilty' acts on the other is particularly interesting. It would appear that a 'criminal' or 'guilty' act is one that looks *manifestly criminal*. (This cannot refer to actual crimes. The defendant stabbing the pillow believing he is stabbing his victim commits no offence if it is his own bedding and pillow that he is damaging. Yet Lord Roskill clearly held that there would be liability for attempt in such a situation.) Fletcher (1978) states that 'manifestly criminal' activities must exhibit at least the following essential features. First, the criminal act must manifest, on its face, the actor's criminal purpose. And secondly, the conduct should be 'of a type that is unnerving and disturbing to the community as a whole'. These requirements are clearly satisfied in the pickpocket and defendant stabbing the pillow cases. The actions manifest the defendant's unlawful purpose and are 'unnerving and disturbing' to the community. This requirement of manifest criminality is, of course, one that lays emphasis on *harm*, albeit of a second-order nature. It insists that actions infringe another's security interests; they must seemingly pose real and objective threats of harm.

On the other hand, 'objectively innocent' activities such as those

111

of Mrs Ryan or the defendant having sexual intercourse with the sixteen-year-old girl believing her to be under sixteen pose no threat of harm to anyone. Nobody's security interests are being violated thereby. If criminal liability were to be imposed in such cases it would be in the complete absence of any degree of harm, however defined. On this basis it can be suggested that the House of Lords in *Anderton v. Ryan* (1985), despite blatantly ignoring Parliament's intentions and creating confused distinctions, did lend its weight to the view here advanced that the causing of harm is an essential prerequisite in the general formula for the construction of criminal liability.

However, in a remarkable *volte-face* the House in *Shivpuri* (1986) overruled its recent decision in *Anderton v. Ryan* (1985) holding that there *could* be criminal liability in *all* such cases of attempting the impossible. This case concerned a defendant charged under section 1 of the Criminal Attempts Act 1981 with attempting to commit the offence of being knowingly concerned in dealing with and harbouring prohibited drugs, contrary to section 170(1)(b) of the Customs and Excise Management Act 1979. The defendant had thought he was dealing in prohibited drugs but it transpired that the substance in his possession was only snuff or similarly harmless vegetable matter. Holding that his own distinction between 'objectively innocent' and 'guilty' actions was 'incapable of sensible application', Lord Bridge proceeded to hold that the defendant's actions were more than merely preparatory to the *intended* offence. Because of section 1(2) it was unnecessary to establish that the actions were more than merely preparatory to the *actual* offence.

This decision must be welcomed on the grounds that it has introduced certainty and simplicity into the law and has given effect to the legislative intent behind the Criminal Attempts Act 1981. However, one can only feel unease at the manner in which the decision was reached. It is abundantly plain that the House of Lords was faced with a situation in *Anderton v. Ryan* (1985) where they felt that criminal liability was inappropriate. People who purchase cheap videos thinking that they are stolen when in fact they are not have done nothing *wrong* other than commit a crime in their minds. On the other hand, the House found itself faced with a defendant in

Shivpuri (1986) whom they felt clearly had done wrong and deserved punishment. He had agreed in India to receive a suitcase of drugs in England that would be delivered to him by a courier. This he did and then, removing one package from the suitcase, he took it, still following instructions, to a railway station to deliver to a third party. He was there arrested. While one can understand the House of Lords' desire to uphold the conviction in such an obvious case of trafficking in 'drugs', one nevertheless wonders whether important legal principles ought to be altered so freely to meet the exigencies of the case before the court.

A more substantial reservation goes to the heart of the theme of this chapter. The approach adopted by the House in *Shivpuri* (1986) (along with the philosophy underlying the Criminal Attempts Act 1981) represents 'subjectivism' gone mad. It amounts to no more than punishing people for their guilty intentions. The man who takes his own umbrella thinking it belongs to another can now be convicted of attempted theft. The Law Commission (Law Commission, 1980) anticipated such problems. Conceding that there would be liability in this situation and in the case of a person buying goods at such a low price that he believed them to be stolen when in fact they were not, they concluded that 'in neither case would it be realistic to suppose that a complaint would be made or that a prosecution would ensue'. This prognosis sadly turned out to be false. *Anderton v. Ryan* (1985) was exactly such a case. A prosecution was brought and under the law as interpreted in *Shivpuri* (1986) criminal liability would ensue. It must surely be a matter of deep regret that English law is now involved in punishing thought-crime. A clearer understanding of the importance of the causing of harm (albeit 'second-order' harm) would have ensured some check on unbridled 'subjectivism' and would have prevented the present situation arising.

4. Conduct Crimes

It will be recalled that while 'result crimes' necessitate proof that the defendant's actions have caused the forbidden harm, there are a substantial number of 'conduct crimes' in which certain conduct is in itself made criminal – irrespective of whether such conduct causes any ulterior harm (see earlier, page 22).

Most of these 'conduct crimes' can be subjected to an analysis similar to that outlined in relation to attempts, as the following two examples illustrate. First, the offence of reckless driving contrary to section 2 of the Road Traffic Act 1972 does in itself constitute a 'second-order' harm; it presents a real threat or risk of actual harm to others. But it is indisputably a lesser offence than causing death by reckless driving contrary to section 3 of the same Act. The direct harm of causing death aggravates the offence.

Secondly, the 'conduct crime' of possessing a firearm without a firearms certificate contrary to section 1 of the Firearms Act 1968 again constitutes in itself a 'second-order' harm. The mere unauthorised possession of such firearms poses a threat of real harm to all of us. Firearms are inherently dangerous and their widespread, unlicensed possession would lead to an increase in their usage in everyday situations – domestic quarrels, children playing with their parents' weapons and so on. Also, the task of the police is made more difficult if householders are permitted their own ' "do-it-yourself" crime-prevention instruments' (Feinberg, 1984). But again, this is a lesser harm (and thus a lesser offence) than *using* such a gun to injure another. Arguably, there is a 'middle' harm between mere possession and actual injury to another – namely, simple unauthorised use thereof, albeit without causing an injury. Such *usage* generates a graver threat to society than mere possession and thus constitutes a more serious harm. This point has been accepted in the United States where many states have general offences of 'reckless endangerment' covering the reckless pointing or firing of a firearm in the direction of another. English law has no such general offence but where a defendant charged with unlawful possession of a firearm has actually fired that gun in a blameworthy manner he will generally receive an increased punishment (*Pennifold and Naylor*, 1974).

5. Conclusion

It thus seems clear that harm is generally a fundamental component in the construction of criminal liability. Clearly, too, there are degrees of harm: some harms are worse than others. And it is submitted that the causing and degree of harm is more than pure 'chance'. Harm is fundamental to our moral assessment of events and thus ought to be an integral component in the structuring of levels of criminal liability and punishment.

3

Major Crimes

A. INTRODUCTION

Having examined how criminal liability is generally constructed, we are now in a position to understand the operation of these general principles in relation to specific crimes.

There is a myriad of offences in English law ranging all the way from murder to mislabelling a can of beans. There are crimes aimed at protecting personal safety (murder, assault, rape etc.), protecting interests in property (theft, fraud, criminal damage etc.), protecting public order (riot, violent disorder etc.), protecting the security of the state (treason, official secrets etc.), protecting public morals (bigamy, obscenity etc.), protecting the administration of justice (perjury, contempt of court etc.) and so on. And then there are the countless regulatory offences aimed at protecting employees, consumers, the environment – and so the list continues.

It has been estimated that there are over 7,200 criminal offences in English law (Justice, 1980). It would of course be impossible and quite beyond the function of this book to explore all these offences. The object here is not to provide a complete synopsis of the law, but rather to explore the underlying principles, themes and purposes of the criminal law in our society today. The best way of achieving this purpose is to focus only on some of the major crimes – namely, offences against the person (sexual and non-sexual), homicide and some property offences.

But even in relation to these chosen offences it must be stressed that the aim is not to provide a complete summary of the law. The major interest will be in exploring the structure of such offences (for example, the relationship of murder to manslaughter) and how this structure (with concomitant levels of punishment) reflects the differing weights attached to the essential components of criminal liability – blame and harm.

B. OFFENCES AGAINST THE PERSON (NON-SEXUAL)

1. Introduction

Even in the area of non-sexual, non-fatal offences against the person there are numerous criminal offences: such as administering poison, false imprisonment, kidnapping – plus other more esoteric offences such as obstructing or assaulting a clergyman in the discharge of his duties or setting mantraps with intent to inflict grievous bodily harm. Again, selectivity is necessary and the primary focus in this section will be on the main offences covering the infliction of violence upon others.

2. The Main Offences

These offences can be ranked in hierarchical order starting with the least serious and progressing upwards in order of seriousness (and in terms of the penalties attached).

At the bottom of the structure lie two separate offences: technical assault and battery – known generically and somewhat loosely as 'common assaults' – both punishable on indictment by a maximum of one year's imprisonment and by a maximum of two months' imprisonment on summary conviction.

A *technical assault* is committed when the defendant intentionally or recklessly causes the victim to apprehend immediate force. So if the defendant raises his fist and threatens to punch the victim, a technical assault is committed. The victim has been made to apprehend immediate unlawful personal violence (*actus reus*); the defendant meant to cause such apprehension or was reckless thereto (*mens rea*). A technical assault is thus similar to an attempt in that there is no physical harm caused to the victim. But with a technical assault there is a direct harm: the fear or apprehension of immediate violence. With an attempt, on the other hand, there need be no such fear – the victim could be unaware that the defendant is attempting to inflict violence upon him.

The object of the offence of technical assault is not to protect people from threats of future violence. Indeed, the criminal law does not provide such protection at all unless there is a threat to kill (Offences against the Person Act 1861, section 16, as amended by the Criminal Law Act 1977, schedule 12). Thus a defendant may with impunity threaten to cut off his victim's fingers or pull his fingernails out the following day. This is a serious gap in the law. The fear and apprehension caused in such cases could be far greater than with many threats of immediate lesser force. While the time-gap allows the victim an opportunity to seek official protection, such protection will in most cases be inadequate to guarantee the victim's safety. The harm (fear and apprehension) is felt to be so significant in such cases that the Law Commission in their Draft Criminal Code have proposed criminalising such threats to cause serious injury (Law Commission, 1985, cl. 68).

Mindful of such considerations and the fact that the essence of (and the harm in) a technical assault is the fear generated by the defendant's threatened violence, the courts have adopted a flexible approach to the requirement that the victim must apprehend *immediate* violence. In *Smith v. Chief Superintendent, Woking Police Station* (1983) it was held that a woman had been assaulted when she saw the defendant looking through her closed bedsitting room window at 11 p.m. Although he was outside her room and would have had to break or force open her window and climb in before he could actually inflict violence upon her (giving her time to run away), it was held that she had apprehended a sufficiently immediate application of force.

The other species of 'common assault' is a *battery*. A battery is the intentional or reckless infliction of unlawful personal force by one person upon another. Here the force must actually be inflicted as opposed to being merely threatened. The term 'force' is somewhat misleading. All that is required for a battery is that the defendant touch the victim without consent or without any other lawful excuse. While the issue is somewhat controversial, the better view is that such a touching must be hostile, rude or threatening (*Wilson v. Pringle*, 1986). We all have a right to personal integrity but if one were simply touched in a non-sexual, non-threatening and non-hostile manner, such invasion of an interest could hardly be sufficiently important to warrant protection via the criminal law.

The touching must be without consent. The law, not surprisingly, implies consent in a whole range of everyday activities: when we run for buses, stand in queues, walk in the street, we all accept that there will be a certain degree of bodily contact and accordingly are deemed to consent thereto. This effectively means we are deemed to submit to all touchings that could be regarded as generally acceptable in the ordinary course of daily life (*Collins v. Wilcock*, 1984).

Moving up the hierarchy, we next find the more serious offence of *assault occasioning actual bodily harm* punishable by a maximum of five years' imprisonment (Offences against the Person Act 1861, section 47). In view of the potential penalty, one would naturally expect that both the degree of harm and blame necessary for this offence would be considerably greater than that required for a common assault. Such expectations are, however, not fulfilled.

The harm required is actual bodily harm – which can indeed be more serious than mere apprehension of violence or a mere touching. But in *Miller* (1954) it was held that actual bodily harm 'includes any hurt or injury calculated to interfere with the health or comfort' of the victim. And in *Taylor v. Granville* (1978) it was decided that a blow to the face must cause some bodily harm, however slight. Thus, presumably, a slap across the face must 'hurt' and must 'interfere with the comfort' of the victim, albeit only for a few moments. It must thus constitute actual bodily harm.

The blame required for this offence is identical to that required for a common assault. All that is required is that the defendant have the *mens rea* of a common assault, i.e. the *mens rea* of either a technical assault or a battery. In *Roberts* (1971) (see earlier, page 103) the defendant tried to pull a coat off his female passenger in his moving car (a common assault). The girl jumped from the car and sustained actual bodily harm. The defendant's argument that he had not intended or foreseen actual bodily harm was rejected. He had the *mens rea* of a common assault and that was all that was necessary.

It seems truly extraordinary that where the blame is constant a much more serious offence and liability to so much greater punishment can result from such a slight increase in harm. This is a classic example of English criminal law at its most incoherent. Coherence in this regard could easily be achieved by reorganising the relative importance of the main components of criminal liability, blame and harm, and by attaching appropriate weight to each of these factors.

The next offence in the structure is *malicious wounding or inflicting grievous bodily harm* (Offences against the Person Act 1861, section 20). The defendant's conduct must result in a wound (the inner and outer skin must be broken) or the infliction of grievous bodily harm ('really serious bodily harm' – *DPP v. Smith*, 1961). In some cases, of course, a wound need not be very serious. Particularly with the advances of modern medical science one can only wonder at the significance of 'wounding' in itself. A wound can be either actual or serious bodily harm and ought logically to be treated as such without any special significance of its own. However, many wounds and certainly all forms of grievous bodily harm do constitute more serious harms than those required for actual bodily harm.

A higher degree of blame is also required for section 20. The defendant must act 'maliciously', which has been interpreted to mean that he must himself foresee the risk of *some* harm occurring; he need not foresee serious harm resulting (*Mowatt*, 1967; *Grimshaw*, 1984). The courts have eschewed the idea that 'maliciously' should be interpreted in the light of *Caldwell* (1982) – despite the fact that prior to *Caldwell* (1982) it was well accepted that 'maliciously' was no more than an old-fashioned synonym for recklessness. Now, however, wishing to circumvent *Caldwell* (1982), the courts have carefully emphasised that 'maliciously' and 'recklessly' are quite separate concepts with separate meanings (*W (a minor) v. Dolbey*, 1983).

Section 20 is thus clearly meant to be a more serious offence than section 47: a greater level of harm and a higher degree of blame is required, yet the maximum penalty for section 20 is five years' imprisonment – exactly the same maximum as for section 47! This absurdity underlines yet again the basic incoherence and confusion underlying the structure of offences against the person.

At the apex of the hierarchy lies *wounding and causing grievous bodily harm with intent* (Offences against the Person Act 1861, section 18). This is a serious offence punishable with a maximum of life imprisonment – yet the harm that needs to be caused is identical to that necessary for section 20, namely, a wounding or grievous bodily harm. What distinguishes the two offences is their differing *mens rea* requirements. For section 18 the defendant must actually *intend* to cause grievous bodily harm or, alternatively, must intend to resist or prevent the lawful apprehension or detainer of any person. Given that the harm is constant for the two offences, it is rather dubious whether their differing blame requirements justify such an enormous differential in terms of available punishments.

3. Conclusion

The picture that emerges is one of chaos. There is almost universal agreement that these offences need to be restructured completely so as to represent a true hierarchy of seriousness with appropriate levels of punishment attached thereto. The leading law reform proposal is that of the Criminal Law Revision Committee (1980) carried forward into the Draft Criminal Code (Law Commission, 1985). This proposal would involve a retention of the present law on common assault but an overhaul of the remaining offences as follows:

(i)   intentionally causing serious injury (maximum of life imprisonment)
(ii) recklessly causing serious injury (maximum of five years' imprisonment)
(iii) intentionally or recklessly causing injury (maximum of three years' imprisonment)

Such a proposal is clearly an improvement on the present law, but is one that pays insufficient attention to the varying degrees of harm and blame. There are obviously more levels of injury than the above proposal suggests. Is a broken nose (clearly serious bodily harm –

Saunders, 1985) which is straightened, leaving no lasting disfigurement or impairment of function, really on a par with serious injuries from which a victim never recovers consciousness (but does not die) or cases where the victim is permanently disabled and is confined to bed or only mobile in a wheelchair for the rest of his life? The argument seems strong that a more subtle restructuring of these offences in terms of harm is required, involving, in order of seriousness: serious injury which is permanently crippling or disfiguring; serious injury of a temporary nature; injury; aggressive force (i.e. 'touchings' of a hostile or threatening nature) and apprehension of immediate force.

Again, more precise fine-tuning is required with regard to the blame component. The Draft Criminal Code distinguishes intentionally causing serious injury from recklessly causing serious injury (with a huge differential in maximum penalty), yet does not distinguish intentionally causing injury from recklessly causing injury. Such an approach is indefensible. It is widely accepted that it is worse (in moral terms) to cause a harm intentionally than to cause it recklessly (see earlier, pages 59–60). The law simply cannot afford to ignore such basic moral distinctions.

And what is meant by 'recklessly' in this context? The Draft Criminal Code assigns this concept its subjective pre-*Caldwell* (1982) meaning. But what of the other indicators of blame – particularly recklessness as defined by *Caldwell* (1982) (effectively the equivalent of gross negligence)? If acting in such a manner is indicative of blame for so many other offences, there is surely no case for excluding personal injuries. A person who fails to consider an obvious risk and thereby causes criminal damage is liable. On this basis a person who fails to consider an obvious risk and thereby causes serious injuries to the victim surely ought to be liable also. The degree of liability and extent of punishment ought probably to be *less* when someone has failed to consider risks as opposed to consciously running them. From this it follows that there ought to be three levels of blame: *intentionally* bringing about the harm; *recklessly* (subjective) bringing about the harm; and *negligently* bringing about the harm (a case can be made here that only *gross negligence* ought to suffice).

But what of the other indicators of blame? We saw earlier how in certain circumstances the law blames people who might lack *mens rea* but whose conduct or condition is regarded by the law as totally unacceptable (and hence blameworthy). The law blames the defendant in *Brennan v. HM Advocate* (1977) for getting himself so intoxicated that he killed his father. The law can blame a diabetic defendant who is at fault in bringing on his own automatism (*Quick and Paddison*, 1973). In such cases where a defendant fails to establish a valid defence he is in effect being punished for his negligence: he ought not to have become so drunk; he ought not to have abstained from food after taking insulin, and so on. On this basis, of the three basic levels of blame, such actors ought to be classified with those who have negligently brought about a harm.

Once it is accepted that there are degrees of harm and levels of blame and that these differing levels need to be reflected by the law (with appropriate levels of punishment), the method of restructuring the offences against the person becomes clear. Appropriate weight must be given to each of these key elements (equal weighting as neither can be regarded as predominant – see earlier, pages 106–8). Their conjunction will then reveal an appropriate level of criminal liability and punishment. (For a detailed table indicating how such a restructured hierarchy could operate, see Clarkson and Keating, 1984.)

A final possibility deserves mention. Are the already suggested indicators of blame and harm the only relevant factors in structuring a hierarchy of offences against the person? Could it not be argued that the following factors have a moral relevance: the circumstances of the crime (for example, prolonged torture in inflicting the injuries); the identity of the victim (for example, mugging an elderly lady or [for quite different and largely deterrent reasons] assaulting a police officer in the execution of his duties – Police Act 1964, section 51); or the identity of the defendant (for example, that he is a person abusing a position of trust in inflicting the injuries)? Along such lines Gordon (1978) states that in Scottish law assaults may be aggravated in the following ways:

1. by the weapon used
2. by the injury caused
3. by the place of assault

4. by the character of the victim which may be
   (a) absolute character (for example, an officer of the law),
   or (b) relative character (for example, parents injuring their children)
5. by the accused's intention.

It is not being argued here that all such factors are sufficiently morally relevant to be incorporated into a reformed structure of offences against the person. But what is being urged is that a less blinkered approach be adopted. Factors other than *mens rea* and direct physical injury should be carefully considered to ascertain whether their existence indicates that the defendant is more blameworthy or has caused a greater degree of harm – and, if so, such factors ought to be utilised as indicators of the appropriate level of blame or harm.

C. SEXUAL OFFENCES

1. Introduction

Many of the non-sexual offences against the person discussed in the previous section could have been committed with a sexual motive and could have involved a variety of harms other than purely physical ones. The victim in *Roberts* (1971), for instance, sustained her injuries in trying to escape from a sexual attack and would almost certainly have suffered mental anguish in addition to her physical injuries. However, the main emphasis there was on physical harm – a harm that is easily capable of ascertainment and gradation in terms of seriousness.

With 'sexual offences', on the other hand, the focus is on the unacceptable conduct of the defendant and not on any physical injury that might be caused. Further, while many sexual offences might well be psychologically damaging to the victim (and this might be the ultimate rationale of some of them), it is unnecessary to prove such injury. If the defendant committed the prohibited act with the requisite degree of blameworthiness, he is liable. (Such offences are thus 'conduct crimes' – see earlier, page 22.)

The 'harm' involved in such offences varies enormously, making it difficult to develop a coherent 'structure' of such offences; comparisons between them are not always easily made. Basically, 'sexual offences' can be grouped into three classes.

First, there is non-consensual sexual aggression which covers offences such as rape and indecent assault. The harm here is the violation of another's interests in bodily security, autonomy and privacy. In addition, such offences can involve degradation, humiliation and psychological trauma.

Secondly, there are offences aimed at protecting the vulnerable – children and mental defectives. For instance, girls under sixteen cannot consent to sexual intercourse. While it has been suggested that this rule exists to protect the interests of parents in having a chaste daughter(!), the better rationale is that the law is here concerned with protecting the immature from the risks of psychological harm that are believed to result from sexual intercourse before attaining a sufficient degree of sexual maturity (an unproven assumption, incidentally).

Thirdly, there is an alarming array of sexual offences whose main rationale is primarily to preserve 'accepted standards of morality'. Thus if a man and his consenting wife commit buggery together both have committed a criminal offence carrying a maximum punishment of life imprisonment! (Sexual Offences Act 1956, section 12(1).) Where both are willing, consenting parties, the main harm the law is concerned with is harm to the moral fabric of society. Other sexual offences of this class include incest, consensual buggery or gross indecency between men in circumstances where the Sexual Offences Act 1967, section 1, does not apply (this Act 'legalised' private homosexual activities between consenting men over the age of twenty-one); the various criminal offences remaining that relate to prostitution, indecent exposure at common law (there is arguably no need to prove the exposure was actually witnessed by anyone, indicating that offensiveness is not the essence of the offence) and buggery with animals (bestiality). The crime of bigamy can possibly be added to this list; there is a direct harm to a victim here: the bigamist's first spouse and his new 'spouse' if the latter is unaware of the bigamy have certainly been harmed; however, the law's primary concern here seems to be protection of the institution of marriage as a basic unit in our society; the offence involves 'an outrage on public decency and morals' (*Allen*, 1872). Finally, the law relating to consent illustrates the law's concern with morality in this field. In *Donovan* (1934) it was held that one could not consent to the infliction of bodily harm if the purpose for which the force was inflicted was disapproved of – in this case, a sado-masochistic 'spanking'. On this basis, flagellation and all other sado-masochistic activities are unlawful if they result in the infliction of any physical harm. In these cases the victim is consenting. While, arguably, the law here is protecting such persons from themselves, the more obvious and generally accepted rationale of such law is that it is aimed at upholding morality in society.

Such 'victimless' or consensual offences raise their own particular problems – in particular, whether they ought to be criminalised at all. This matter will be considered later (pages 167–77). Selectivity again being necessary in order to sharpen the focus, the remainder of this section will be devoted to the first category of sexual offences mentioned above, namely, offences of sexual aggression or violence directed at non-consenting adults.

2. The Main Offences

Four such offences will be considered: indecent exposure under the Vagrancy Act 1824, indecent assault, buggery and rape. Indecent exposure and rape can only be committed against women. The victim of an indecent assault or buggery may be either male or female.

Under section 4 of the Vagrancy Act 1824 the offence of *indecent exposure* is committed when a man wilfully and indecently exposes his penis with the intention of insulting any female. The exposure need not be in a public place. The offence is triable only summarily and punishable with three months' imprisonment. This can be regarded as an offence of sexual aggression against women. The underlying 'harm' is the fear, apprehension or disgust felt by a woman so accosted. While a woman might be offended by the exposure of the backside, such exposure presents a far lesser threat of further sexual aggression and thus does not fall within the ambit of

the offence (although such an exposure in public could well constitute the common law offence of indecent exposure which is aimed at
upholding standards of decency).

An *indecent assault* is an assault or a battery committed in circumstances of indecency. Where the victim is a woman the maximum penalty is two years' imprisonment, but where a man is
indecently assaulted the maximum penalty is ten years' imprisonment! Such blatant sexism which appears to regard an invasion of a
male's autonomy over his body as far worse than a comparable
invasion of a woman's autonomy is clearly unacceptable – even
though *in practice* sentences are similar, irrespective of the sex of the
victim.

As the offence may be committed by either a technical assault or a
battery, it is clear that there need be no actual touching provided the
woman apprehends an unlawful touching (*Rolfe*, 1952). Thus the
distinction between indecent exposure and indecent assault can be a
fine one. If the defendant exposes his penis to a woman it will be an
indecent exposure if she does not apprehend being touched, but
indecent assault if she does apprehend such touching. The *mens rea*
distinction can be even finer in such cases. For indecent exposure the
defendant must intend to insult the woman; for indecent assault he
must intend (or be reckless) to make her apprehend an indecent
touching.

The assault or battery must be committed in circumstances of
indecency, which means there must be something *overtly* sexual in
the assault. In *George* (1956) the defendant attempted to remove a
girl's shoe; being a 'shoe fetishist', he obtained sexual gratification
from such activities. It was held that this was not an indecent assault
as the actions were not overtly sexual. But as long as the assault is
overtly sexual it can take almost any form including bottom-
pinching and, perhaps, even a kiss. Most such offences, however, do
involve some form of touching of the genitals.

The crime of *buggery* is committed when a man has anal intercourse with a woman (irrespective of her consent) or with another
man (unless the buggery is committed in private between two consenting males over the age of twenty-one – Sexual Offences Act
1967, section 1). Anal penetration must be established; emission is

irrelevant. Non-consensual buggery with a man is punishable by a maximum of ten years' imprisonment, but such buggery with a woman carries a maximum penalty of life imprisonment! Such discrimination is, again, quite indefensible. Where the victim is a man there is thus no difference in severity of penalty between an indecent assault and forcible buggery.

The sexual offence that has attracted by far the most public attention is that of *rape*. This offence, punishable by a maximum of life imprisonment, is committed when a man has unlawful sexual intercourse with a woman who does not consent to the intercourse; the defendant must know she is not consenting to the intercourse or be reckless as to whether she is consenting (Sexual Offences (Amendment) Act 1976, section 1(1)).

The sexual intercourse (penetration of the vagina with the penis) must be 'unlawful' which in this context means outside marriage. By virtue of marriage a wife is deemed to consent to sexual intercourse and therefore during the marriage the husband cannot rape his wife (in law) even though in reality the wife does not consent. The only exceptions to this rule are when it has been made plain by a court order or its equivalent that the wife's consent to intercourse has been revoked, for example, a decree of judicial separation or an injunction restraining the husband from molesting the wife (*Steele*, 1977). The uninitiated might be forgiven for thinking that this rule is no more than a barbarous relic of the morality of an earlier age, yet the Criminal Law Revision Committee (1984) has recommended its retention, at least where husband and wife are still cohabiting. Their argument is essentially that there would be immense evidential problems in establishing rape in such cases, and such matters are best left to matrimonial law rather than the criminal law. It nevertheless does seem extraordinary that in a modern so-called civilised society that is in many respects committed to the goal of equality between the sexes, a married woman should be denied full control and autonomy over her own body. It has been stated that 'the criminal law should express the way we live' (Fletcher, 1978). We surely do not live in an age in which a wife can simply be regarded as a sexual plaything of the husband with whom he can have intercourse as he likes, irrespective of her consent.

The unlawful sexual intercourse must be without consent. This gives rise to enormous evidential problems as defendants commonly claim that the woman was consenting and it can be extremely difficult to establish this point one way or the other in court. This can result in extremely humiliating and distressing cross-examination of the woman in court (and similarly distressing interrogation prior to that). Nevertheless, establishing her lack of consent is crucial: it is what transforms the totally innocent and much indulged-in activity of sexual intercourse into the very serious crime of rape.

It used to be thought that what was necessary was that the woman did not consent to the penetration of the penis. However, in *Kaitamaki* (1984) it was held that rape was committed if the woman was not consenting at any time during intercourse. Thus, even though she consented to penetration, if during the intercourse she revoked her consent and advised the man thereof but he persisted in the intercourse, this would be rape. This is a difficult decision. Clearly, a woman by consenting initially to intercourse cannot be 'estopped' from later revoking the consent; the intercourse could be causing her great pain and distress. Nevertheless, one cannot help feeling that while such a man should be guilty of some offence, it should not be rape. The woman has consented to the man inserting his penis into her vagina. Her degree of emotional and psychological trauma is not the same as other women who never so consented. The crime and label 'rape' should be reserved for these worst cases where consent to penetration was never given.

As indicated earlier, the requisite degree of blameworthiness, in the form of *mens rea*, for rape is spelled out by the Sexual Offences (Amendment) Act 1976, section 1(1). The defendant must *know* the woman is not consenting or must be *reckless* as to whether she is consenting. Section 1(2) of this Act endorses a subjective test: the question is whether the defendant actually believes the woman is consenting; the reasonableness of his belief is only important in evidential terms. It thus appears that there is no room for the objective test of recklessness as laid down in *Caldwell* (1982) (*Satnam and Kewal*, 1984). No matter how absurd the defendant's mistake, if he honestly believed the woman was consenting (and if the jury believe him) he will not be guilty of rape. Again, the wisdom of such an approach can be queried. The man's mistake here is easily avoided. If there is the slightest doubt as to whether the woman is consenting, he should ask her. He will, after all, be close enough to do so easily! Failure to make such an enquiry indicates a lack of concern for a woman's bodily integrity. Failure to take the requisite care when it could so easily be taken is surely blameworthy – and when it results in such a major harm as a violation of a woman's autonomy over her own body then this is surely sufficient to justify the moral condemnation of the criminal law.

3. Conclusion

As with the non-sexual offences against the person, the structure of the above sexual offences could be seen to be incoherent. Is rape (maximum of life imprisonment) *always* that much more serious than indecent assault on a woman (maximum of two years)? Is penetration of the vagina by the penis necessarily so much more reprehensible than prolonged and painful penetration of the vagina or the anus by a bottle or broomhandle or than forcible fellatio? Is it always so much worse than many of the other humiliating and degrading indecent assaults that can include defecating or urinating upon a woman?

The common denominator of these sexual offences is not so much that they are committed through a desire for sexual gratification, but rather that they represent an assertion of power by a man wanting dominance and humiliation over his victim. Such offences cause terror and the psychological degradation of being treated as an 'object' to be used at the whim of the man (Queen's Bench Foundation, 1976).

Given this common denominator which can be perceived as one of the main harms involved in the above offences, one is forced to ask whether it is necessary to retain the distinction between such offences. Why not abolish these individual crimes and substitute a single broad offence of unlawful sexual assault? The judge would then be able to tailor the sentence to fit the individual facts of the case before him and thus take account of the reality that these offences vary enormously in terms of seriousness. Canadian law has introduced a broadly drawn single offence of sexual assault. This offence can become aggravated (and thus carry a higher potential penalty) – but only on the basis of the degree of physical injury caused (Criminal Law Amendment Act, S.C. 1980–81–82, c. 125).

There are two main (and, it is submitted, insurmountable) objections to such a proposal. First, it would lead to an unacceptable increase in judicial discretion in sentencing. We shall see later (pages 193–4) that such discretion has come under sharp attack in recent years. Law reform proposals that *hugely* increase such discretionary powers must be rejected. Secondly, such a broadly drawn offence would be morally uninformative. Criminal offences are categorised and labelled for symbolic reasons. The category and label 'rape' (with its severe penalty), for instance, is used to emphasise the utter reprehensibility of such conduct; it is employed to convey the symbolic message to the public that such activity is the 'worst' form of sexual misconduct. A new broad offence, unlawful sexual conduct, which encompassed both the rapist and the bottom-pincher, would convey a distorted message as to the degree of societal rejection of the activity involved.

An alternative could be to follow the solution adopted in Minnesota where the individual sexual offences have been replaced by a single offence of 'criminal sexual conduct', but this offence has been subdivided into four degrees, each degree representing a different level of seriousness and carrying its own penalty. Several factors are utilised in distinguishing between the four degrees – such as causing personal injury to the victim or being armed with a dangerous weapon. But the most important distinguishing feature is that drawn between 'sexual penetration' and 'sexual contact' – the former aggravating the offence. 'Sexual penetration' is defined as including any intrusion into the victim's 'genital or anal openings' by any part of the defendant's body (penis or hand etc.) or by any object. Thus there is no distinction drawn between vaginal and anal penetration and it does not matter whether the penetration is by the defendant's penis or other object. 'Sexual contact', on the other hand, is touching the victim's 'intimate parts' for the purpose of satisfying the defendant's 'sexual or aggressive impulses' (Minn. Stat. Ann., sections 609.341–609.345).

Such an approach is clearly an improvement on the notion of having a single broad offence. Nevertheless, it is submitted that English law should (and will) retain its present distinctive offences of rape, buggery and indecent assault. Take rape, for instance. There are several reasons for regarding rape as a distinctive offence. The non-consensual intrusion of a man's penis into the vagina represents the ultimate in invasion of a woman's privacy and autonomy. Our society attaches a very special significance to vaginal intercourse, 'the ultimate sexual act'. Rape debases the activity. It is like sacrilege to 'sacred' sexual intercourse. Similarly, and for related reasons, a woman's vagina is regarded as her most private and 'special' part. Rape involves an intrusion into this most private domain by the very symbol of male aggressiveness, the penis. While the physical pain might be greater with the insertion of a bottle or other such object, it is penis penetration that is regarded as specially significant: it is the ultimate assertion of male power. The woman is having to suffer the most intimate proximity possible between herself and her assailant – a proximity not only degrading in itself, but one that creates a fear of venereal disease and pregnancy. And finally, there are the traumatising after-effects of rape which can make women fearful of sexual intercourse for years, if not for ever.

For all these related reasons it would appear that the case for retaining rape as a special offence is overwhelming. The public understand what 'rape' is. The law should not stray too far from reflecting such common understanding.

Similar arguments can be used in relation to buggery. While it is possible to regard buggery as simply an aggravated form of sexual assault, there is a strong case for retaining this crime in its present form. Most people would regard non-consensual anal penetration by the penis as significantly more serious than other forms of sexual assault. The special degradation and humiliation of such activity coupled with the risk of disease, especially AIDS, suggests retention of buggery as a separate offence.

One final possibility deserves brief mention. If we are going to retain rape, buggery and indecent assault as separate offences, are not these offences, or at least some of them, too broad? Indecent assault, for instance, covers a wide range of conduct from bottom-pinching to vaginal penetration with a broomstick. Should not such a broad offence be subdivided into degrees, each with its own maximum penalty? Such a solution, commonly employed in the United States, has been seriously considered in this country (Criminal Law Revision Committee, 15th Report, 1984) but the main problem is achieving agreement on the criteria for distinguishing between the different degrees of such an offence. Should first-degree indecent assault be limited to indecent assaults involving 'penetration' (by bottle, stick, hand etc.)? Or, should we adopt the solution employed by the Australian State of Victoria that the more serious offence is only established if the indecent assault is accompanied by an aggravating circumstance from a specified list, for example, inflicting serious personal violence upon the victim or doing an act which seriously degrades or humiliates the victim (Crimes (Sexual Offences) Act 1980, section 46(1)).

While agreement on such fundamental matters might be difficult to achieve, it ought not to be impossible. Such an approach would have the further advantage of reducing the present wide discretionary sentencing powers of the judges (see later, pages 193–4). However, this idea of subdividing offences into degrees is by no means limited to sexual offences. If anything, the arguments for such subcategorisation are even stronger in the field of homicide offences and, accordingly, this proposal will be returned to in the following section.

D. HOMICIDE

1. Introduction

There are three categories of homicide in English law: murder, manslaughter (of which there are several species) and infanticide.

In structuring offences against the person and sexual offences we saw that the law was concerned to balance the differing harms that could occur with the differing degrees of blameworthiness that could accompany the defendant's actions. With homicide offences, on the other hand, one is dealing with a constant harm, namely, the death of the victim. Accordingly, homicide offences have been graded primarily in terms of blameworthiness. Take, for instance, the distinction between the two main homicide offences, murder and manslaughter. The *actus reus* of these two offences is identical: the defendant must unlawfully kill the victim. But what distinguishes them is the different level of blameworthiness required for each. Murder is committed when the defendant unlawfully kills his victim with *malice aforethought*. Manslaughter is such an unlawful killing *without malice aforethought* but with a different and lesser degree of blameworthiness.

2. The Offences

The most serious of the homicide offences is *murder*. The very word 'murder' encapsulates all our moral beliefs as to the dreadful and terrible nature of the crime. Murderers are immortalised in our museums and literature; their trials are publicised and dramatised in our daily press; they have committed the ultimate and irreversible harm of taking away another's life; they have committed a 'crime like no other'; the maximum wrath of society is visited upon them – previously the death penalty and now the fixed sentence of life imprisonment, a sentence that *must* be imposed upon all murderers.

Such emotive 'reasoning' causes little dissent when dealing with the paradigmatic cases of murder, such as those of Peter Sutcliffe or Denis Nilsen. Their horrendous crimes are rightly stigmatised as murder. The real problem, as far as the law is concerned, arises in those cases where the defendant has killed but claims that he did not mean to do so. The defendant in *Hyam* (1975) (see earlier, page 59) realised that her actions could cause serious injuries or death to her victims but she was not trying to kill. The two most recent House of Lords cases are similar. In *Moloney* (1985) the defendant and his stepfather, who had both been drinking fairly heavily, engaged in a 'ridiculous challenge' to ascertain who was quicker on the draw with a shotgun. The defendant claimed that he did not aim the gun but simply pulled the trigger. The stepfather was killed. Here his purpose was to be quickest on the draw and at firing the gun. Death or serious injury was, however, a very likely consequence of such actions. In *Hancock* (1986) two striking miners pushed a large lump of concrete from a bridge on to the convoy of cars below carrying a miner to work. The concrete struck a taxi's windscreen and killed the driver. The defendants claimed they had not meant to kill or cause serious injury. Their plan was to drop the concrete in the middle lane of the carriageway (the convoy being in the nearside lane). Their aim had been to block the road and frighten the miner in order to prevent him getting to work.

The defendants in these cases were all found guilty of murder at their trials. On appeal, the House of Lords ultimately affirmed the murder conviction in *Hyam* (1975) but reduced the defendants' liability to manslaughter in the other two cases. It is, however, by no means clear that Mrs Hyam was indeed sufficiently blameworthy to be classified as a murderess – or, alternatively, that the defendants in the other two cases deserved to escape liability for murder.

The central problem for the law has thus been one of devising a criterion for distinguishing the worst cases as murder from the remaining unlawful homicides which are classified as manslaughter and carry the lesser stigma and punishment of a *maximum* of life imprisonment (as opposed to mandatory life imprisonment for murder). To effect this classification the law has developed the concept of *malice aforethought*. Only if a defendant kills with this malice aforethought is he sufficiently blameworthy to be classified as a murderer. But what does 'malice aforethought' mean?

Originally the term bore its literal meaning. There had to 'malice' in the sense of spite or ill-will and the killing had to be 'afore-thought' in that it must have been planned or premeditated. However, it was soon realised that this was too narrow a definition for murder and the term 'malice aforethought' was expanded to become a mere technical label, describing those perceived to be sufficiently blameworthy to deserve hanging (or, since 1965, the fixed manda-tory penalty of life imprisonment for murder). This degree of expansion of the concept has varied over the years, such inconsis-tency meaning that a 'murderer' of one year might only be guilty of manslaughter in another year, or vice versa. Mrs Hyam, for instance, was convicted of murder in 1974; today she might well be convicted only of manslaughter.

Nevertheless, despite such variations in precise meaning, it is clear that over the past century, at least, the crime of murder has not been limited to those who kill intentionally. The law has also sought to embrace within the category 'murder' those who have acted with extreme recklessness on the basis that such gross recklessness evidences indifference to the value of human life and a willingness to kill which can be as reprehensible as most intentional killings. In the United States there has been an open articulation of such a view with the Model Penal Code (1962) stating that it is murder to kill another 'recklessly under circumstances manifesting extreme indifference to the value of human life' (section 210.2(1)(b)) but only manslaughter when a criminal homicide is 'committed recklessly' (section 210.3).

In England, however, malice aforethought, the dividing line between murder and manslaughter, had never been openly and honestly defined in such a manner but the law has adopted a variety of devices to try and achieve the same result. Thus it has long been the law that an intention to cause grievous bodily harm suffices for the *mens rea* of murder. The most acceptable rationale of this rule is that a defendant who intends really serious bodily harm is running a grave risk that death might result from his actions; such excessive risk-taking deserves to be punished as murder. Secondly, until 1957, if one killed while engaged in committing a felony which was 'known to be dangerous to life, and likely in itself to cause death' (*Serné*, 1887) one became guilty of murder under the 'felony-murder rule'. This, of course, was simply another way of punishing extreme recklessness. Indeed, under the Model Penal Code's formulation the commission of a listed dangerous felony raises a presumption of the requisite high degree of recklessness required for murder. Thirdly, the law achieved its desired result of punishing gross recklessness as murder by some rather unsubtle semantic trickery. The House of Lords in *DPP v. Smith* (1961) and two of their Lordships in *Hyam* (1975) stated that murder was a 'crime of intention' and then proceeded to give the word 'intention' a meaning broad enough to encompass cases of extreme recklessness. However, two other members of the House of Lords in *Hyam* (1975) (Lords Cross and Kilbrandon) were prepared to rise above such sophistry and admit openly that murder could be committed by gross recklessness and without an intention to kill. The majority in *Hyam* (1975) held that this requisite degree of extreme recklessness for malice aforethought (whatever its formal nomenclature) was satisfied when the defendant foresaw death or grievous bodily harm as a highly probable result of his actions.

Such an approach has been subjected to fierce criticism on two fronts. First, it is argued that intentional killings are morally more reprehensible than killings by gross recklessness and that the special label 'murder' should be reserved for the very worst killings, the intentional killings. Secondly, if the distinction between murder and manslaughter is one between extreme recklessness and recklessness, one is forced to draw very fine lines on the continuum of risk-taking. It is rather like distinguishing between a long piece of string and a very long piece of string. No clear principled basis for the distinction exists. The result is a blurring at the edges of both murder and manslaughter and in this 'grey area' it becomes impossible to predict with any certainty whether defendants like those in *Hyam* (1975) *Moloney* (1985) and *Hancock* (1986) are guilty of murder or manslaughter.

The House of Lords has partially responded to these criticisms. In *Moloney* (1985) the House firmly ruled that murder was a crime of intention. Gross recklessness in the form of foresight would not suffice. The *mens rea* of murder, malice aforethought, requires proof of either an intention to kill or an intention to cause grievous bodily harm. Nothing less will suffice. At first sight such an approach seems attractive and to have simplified the law greatly. However, one is still left with the central problem of defining intention with sufficient precision to enable murder to be distinguished clearly from manslaughter. As was seen earlier (pages 60–2) *Moloney* (1985) and *Hancock* (1986) have left the law on this point in a state of considerable confusion. There is now no general definition of intention, its meaning being entirely a matter for the jury to determine. The result is that the line between murder and manslaughter is more blurred than ever before; it has become even more difficult to predict whether defendants, such as those in the leading cases, are guilty of murder or manslaughter. Reading between the lines, the House of Lords appears determined to have its cake and eat it. Murder is a 'crime of intention' but maximum flexibility is retained by not defining intention to ensure that juries can still legitimately convict of murder those felt to be deserving of that label even if such persons did not actually mean to kill or cause grievous bodily harm. This is an intolerable position. If murder is to be reserved as a crime of intention, intention must be defined so as to demarcate murder from manslaughter. On the other hand, if those who act with gross recklessness are felt to deserve the label 'murder', then this must be stated explicitly. Despite the efforts of the Court of Appeal in *Nedrick* (1986), it is clear that the House of Lords is not going to adopt either course. It is therefore incumbent upon Parliament to take the initiative in this regard.

A final criticism relating to the *mens rea* of murder must be mentioned. If the crime and label 'murder' is to be reserved for the 'worst' killings and if these worst killings are intentional killings, then there is a strong case for arguing that the *mens rea* of murder should be limited to an intention to kill or, at the very least, an intention 'to cause serious injury and being aware that he may kill' (Draft Criminal Code, clause 56). Yet it is clear law that a mere intention to cause grievous bodily harm will suffice for murder (*Cunningham*, 1982). There seems little justification for such an approach. It is difficult to see that this species of risk-taking is any worse or more dangerous than the other forms of risk-taking. Under the present law, if one intends to break one's victim's leg (grievous bodily harm) but instead he is killed, one is guilty of murder. But if one sets fire to a house foreseeing the *death* of the occupants as *likely*, one is only guilty of manslaughter. This is plainly absurd. Either all forms of extreme risk-taking should constitute murder, or none should. One cannot pick and choose between categories of risk-taking in such an indiscriminate manner.

Finally, a brief word needs to be said about the punishment for murder. While all convicted murderers must be sentenced to life imprisonment, they seldom actually remain in prison for their whole lives. The judge, in imposing life imprisonment, can recommend a minimum period which in his view should elapse before the offender can be released. Thus when in *Sutcliffe* (1981), the 'Yorkshire Ripper' was sentenced to life imprisonment for murder, the trial judge recommended that he spend at least thirty years before being considered for release. But in most cases once the judge has sentenced the offender to life imprisonment, the real sentencing power passes to the Parole Board who can, at any stage, recommend the release of the offender. If the Home Secretary accepts this recommendation the offender is released but is never entirely free: for the remainder of his life he is 'on licence', that is, he is subject to supervision by a probation officer and may be recalled to prison at any stage should his conduct give cause for concern and suggest that he might be a threat to society.

Because murders vary considerably – from deliberate cold-blooded killings to 'mercy killings' – it has been argued that the automatic sentence of life imprisonment for all murderers is inappropriate; the judge ought to be able to impose any sentence which would accurately reflect the gravity of the crime. Such a proposal would mean, however, that for most practical purposes there would be little distinction between murder and manslaughter. Whether these two crimes should in fact be merged into one single offence will be considered at the end of this section, after the crime of manslaughter has been examined.

While the crime of murder is meant to be limited to the most reprehensible killings, the crime of *manslaughter* is an extremely broad 'dustbin category' covering most unlawful killings that are not murder. There are several categories of manslaughter each with its own technical rules but all sharing the same common premise that the defendant is blameworthy in some way, but not sufficiently blameworthy to be classified as a murderer. The degree of blame-worthiness can vary enormously; the killing might only just fall short of murder or, alternatively, it might be little more than an accidental killing and only just criminal. These differing degrees of culpability can be reflected by the sentence imposed. The judge may impose any sentence up to a maximum of life imprisonment.

Manslaughters are traditionally classified as being either 'volun-tary' or 'involuntary'. Voluntary manslaughter is committed where the defendant does possess the necessary 'malice aforethought' for murder but he is regarded as having a reduced level of blameworthi-ness because of the existence of a specified excuse, namely, provoca-tion, diminished responsibility or because the killing was pursuant to a suicide pact. (See earlier, pages 81–3.)

Involuntary manslaughter, on the other hand, is regarded as less serious than murder because the defendant does not act with malice aforethought. He has a less blameworthy state of mind – but there must nevertheless be *some* blame. This requisite blame can be established in one of two ways:

First, under the doctrine of *constructive manslaughter*, if the defendant is engaged in committing an *unlawful act* (for example, a common assault) from which death results, the law will readily impose liability insisting only that the unlawful act be slightly dangerous in that it must be *likely* (objectively) *to cause some physical harm*. (This is the successor to the old 'misdemeanour-manslaughter rule' which was the correlative of the old 'felony-murder rule' [see earlier, page 136].) However, any type of criminal unlawful act will now suffice as long as it is criminal *per se*; it must be criminal for some independent reason – and not simply that it is a *prima facie* lawful act (for example, driving) being performed in a negligent manner (*Andrews v. DPP*, 1937). The defendant is blamed for engaging in such a dangerous unlawful act in the first place. If no death resulted he would be blamed and punished for that unlawful act itself. But if his actions have additionally caused the death of another, then this blame, coupled with the aggravated harm, leads to liability for the more serious offence of manslaughter. For instance, in *Larkin* (1943) the defendant brandished a razor at a man in order to terrify him. His drunk mistress fell against the razor, cut her throat and died. Here there was an unlawful act (an assault by intentionally terrifying the man); it was an unlawful act likely to cause some physical harm (brandishing razors at persons who have been drinking heavily must always be dangerous); the defendant was accordingly liable for manslaughter.

The second method of establishing the requisite degree of blame for involuntary manslaughter is by 'reckless manslaughter'. If the defendant is engaged in a *prima facie* lawful activity, such as driving a car or taking care of an aged aunt, from which death results (and legal causation is established), he will be liable for manslaughter only if it is established that he was *'reckless' (Seymour*, 1983; *Kong Cheuk Kwan*, 1986). This requisite recklessness, however, can be established with somewhat surprising ease given the serious nature of the crime of manslaughter. The *Lawrence* (1982) test of recklessness applies (see page 65). Under this it is not necessary to prove that the defendant was aware of the risks; it is enough if he gave *no thought* to the possibility of there being any risks. Further, the risk need not be one of death or serious injury; it is sufficient if there is simply an obvious and serious risk of causing *physical injury* or of doing *substantial damage to property* (*Kong Cheuk Kwan*, 1986). Many commentators regard such a test as unacceptably broad (Smith, 1985). However, the one possible limiting and redeeming feature of the test is that there must be an obvious and *serious* risk, indicating that there must be a very high chance of the physical injury or substantial damage to property occurring. If such a high chance of these consequences occurring does exist and the defendant persists in so acting and as a result kills another person, perhaps liability for manslaughter is not inappropriate.

The final species of manslaughter is *causing death by reckless driving* (section 1 of the Road Traffic Act 1972, as amended). Previously drivers who killed with their motor cars were simply charged with manslaughter. Juries, however, were extremely loath to convict for this offence with its serious stigma. They could relate to such defendants in a way that they could not relate to defendants in other manslaughter cases such as *Larkin* (1943); most jurors drive cars (or are driven by family and friends) but they do not brandish razors in a threatening manner. To try and combat this 'there, but for the grace of God, go I' thinking, Parliament created this new separate offence with a different label and punishable by a maximum of five years' imprisonment.

In *Seymour* (1983) the House of Lords held that the ingredients of this offence were 'identical' to those of reckless manslaughter; the *Lawrence* (1982) test of recklessness applies to both offences. We are thus left with the extraordinary conclusion that a very serious offence carrying a maximum penalty of life imprisonment (manslaughter) is identical in its ingredients to a much lesser offence carrying a maximum penalty of five years' imprisonment (causing death by reckless driving).

The House of Lords in *Jennings* (1982), while also holding that there was no difference in substance between the two offences, indicated that prosecutions for manslaughter would only be appropriate in *very grave cases*. In the absence of any explanation by the judiciary, logic would dictate that 'a very grave case' of causing death by reckless driving would be one where the driving was so bad or where so many people were killed that a sentence in excess of five years' imprisonment might be appropriate. However, a perusal of the sentencing cases on causing death by reckless driving indicates that even in the very worst cases sentences in excess of three years' imprisonment are virtually unheard of. Further, the leading case of *Boswell* (1984) has laid down that in bad cases where 'aggravating circumstances' are present a sentence of 'at least two years' imprisonment' is appropriate. On the basis of this evidence it is hard to imagine the type of 'very grave case' that would justify a prosecution for manslaughter and punishment in excess of five years' imprisonment. Presumably the only cases that would qualify as manslaughter would be those where, as in *Seymour* (1983), the defendant basically uses his motor car as an offensive weapon but lacks the *mens rea* necessary for murder.

A final homicide offence deserves brief mention. Where a mother kills her own child who is under twelve months of age and at the time of the killing 'the balance of her mind was disturbed by reason of not having fully recovered from the effect of giving birth to the child or by reason of the effect of lactation consequent upon the birth of the child' (Infanticide Act 1938, section 1), the mother is guilty of *infanticide* and not murder. This offence carries a maximum penalty of life imprisonment. The rationale of this offence is similar to that of voluntary manslaughter. Such 'disturbed' mothers are regarded as having a partial excuse for their actions (see earlier, page 82); their mental imbalance renders them less blameworthy; less punishment is deserved. (In practice, a probation order is the normal sentence.)

In reality, however, there is virtually no medical evidence to support such a rationale (West, 1965). It appears that most of such babies who are killed are part of the 'battered baby syndrome' whose killers are often suffering from environmental stress, coupled with various personality disorders totally unrelated to the effects of childbirth and lactation. These pressures apply just as strongly to mothers coping with older children and to some fathers – yet no excuse is available in such cases unless the defendant can be brought within the ambit of diminished responsibility (see page 83). On this basis perhaps it would be best if the offence of infanticide were abolished. All mentally unbalanced mothers (and fathers) could then simply plead diminished responsibility if they killed their children (Butler Committee, 1975). This would ensure that the focus was on the excusing condition (the mental abnormality) rather than on the somewhat fortuitous age of the child and sex of the parent.

3. Conclusion

In *Sutcliffe* (1981) both defence and prosecution were content that the notorious 'Yorkshire Ripper' plead guilty to manslaughter. Both knew that a sentence of life imprisonment was inevitable, whatever the verdict. This negotiated plea would have saved much time and money and would have protected the relatives of victims from hitherto unrevealed and unpleasant details of the crimes. The judge, however, declined to accept such a plea, insisting on a full trial which resulted in a murder verdict. To the judge in *Sutcliffe* (1981), and to many others, it was critical that murder be sharply distinguished from manslaughter in order that a clear moral distinction be drawn between the two offences. The very label 'murder', coupled with its fixed sentence of life imprisonment, emphasises the special stigma attached to that crime and underlines the 'dreadfulness' of the offence.

However, critics of the present division between murder and manslaughter complain that, apart from the near impossibility of distinguishing clearly between the two offences, the present categorisation does not distinguish the different species of homicide with sufficient precision. Each offence is simply too broad, encompassing too many different degrees of blameworthiness.

Accordingly, it could be suggested that English law follow the lead set by law in the United States and subdivide both murder and manslaughter into degrees, each level of offence carrying its own penalty. How could this be best achieved?

To date English law has proceeded primarily on the basis that offences should be classified according to the differing mental elements of the defendant. Thus, broadly speaking, murder is distinguished from manslaughter by the presence or absence of an intention to kill or cause grievous bodily harm. Such an approach could be extended. For instance, it is fairly common in the United States for first-degree murder to cover planned, premeditated killings with second-degree murder covering other intentional killings. Manslaughters could be similarly categorised. In New York, for instance, 'intent to cause serious physical injury' is first-degree manslaughter while second-degree manslaughter covers 'recklessly causing death' – and there is an even lesser offence, criminally negligent homicide, extending to killings with 'criminal negligence' (NY Penal Law, sections 125.10–125.20 (McKinney)).

Such proposals are, however, fraught with difficulties and could simply exacerbate the present problem of distinguishing between degrees of *mens rea*. An alternative, bolder approach might be to recognise that levels of blameworthiness are not necessarily totally dependent on differing mental states. Other factors could be relevant. For instance, in New York it is the identity of the victim that is critical in distinguishing first-degree murder (intentionally killing a police officer or an employee of a state correctional institution – NY Penal Law, section 125.27 (McKinney)). Alternatively, the categorisation could be made dependent on the method or circumstances of the killing. Prominent factors in the United States here are: hired killings, murder by poison and murder by torturing one's victim to death. Such an approach has effectively been adopted in England 'via the back door' with the Home Secretary openly adopting a policy, approved by the courts, of ensuring that certain categories of murderers (those who have killed police or prison officers, terrorist killings, murder during robbery or the sadistic or sexual murder of children) will not be released on parole until the expiry of at least twenty years (*Findlay*, 1984). One of the central debates in English criminal law over the next decade should be whether offences such as homicide should be classified almost exclusively in terms of *mens rea* or whether a wider range of factors should be fed into the equation.

A final, more radical, solution has already been the subject of much discussion. Lord Kilbrandon in *Hyam* (1975) suggested that because of the difficulty in distinguishing murder from manslaughter, both crimes should be abolished and replaced by a new single offence of unlawful homicide; the judge would have complete discretion as to sentence and could reflect the exact gravity of the offence in his sentence. Such an approach would have the significant advantage of ensuring that only the 'worst' cases received life imprisonment. Such defendants would *in fact* spend substantial periods of time in prison, thus increasing public confidence in the life sentence rather than the present 'devaluation' of the meaning of a life sentence by the release of some such persons after a short period of time – persons who never deserved the label and punishment for murder in the first place. This approach would also put an end to the present plea-bargaining that occurs – but only occurs in *some* murder cases. And finally, the somewhat odd excuses of provocation, diminished responsibility and suicide pact, which only really exist to ameliorate the harshness of the mandatory penalty for murder, could be abolished and relegated to their proper place – as mitigating factors relevant to sentencing.

Such arguments, however, overlook three insurmountable (it is submitted) objections. First, there is the moral significance and deterrent value attached to the label 'murder'. It is surely not appropriate to lump together under the morally uninformative title 'unlawful homicide' deliberate, cold-blooded killers and 'fools' such as the defendant in *Lamb* (1967). One of the functions of having categories of offences is to communicate to the public the differing degrees of rejection or unacceptability of certain conduct. Such symbolic messages would not be conveyed if the distinction between murder and manslaughter were collapsed.

Secondly, such a new single offence would mean that a judge would receive no guidance from the jury as to important questions of *fact*, such as whether the defendant intended death or was provoked. Such matters would only be relevant in determining the appropriate level of sentence and thus would be left entirely to the judge. Third and finally, such a new offence would greatly increase the judge's discretionary powers of sentencing. We shall see in the final section of this book that over the last decade there has been mounting criticism of such discretionary powers and attempts made at curbing it. With this background, proposals to reform the substantive criminal law in a manner that would significantly increase the judge's discretionary sentencing powers must be unacceptable.

Such a proposal thus looks unlikely to win wide acceptance. Equally, the difficulties involved in drawing clear distinctions between various degrees of murder and manslaughter make those proposals less viable. It seems therefore that English law, for the foreseeable future, will remain committed to its present broad distinction between murder and manslaughter, the line between the two forever shifting to and fro as the tide of public opinion ebbs and flows.

E. PROPERTY OFFENCES

1. Introduction

The political and economic structure of our society depends to a very large extent upon the concept of private property. Thus legal rights and interests in property such as ownership and possession are encouraged and protected. Unauthorised interferences with such rights and interests are seen as threatening the socioeconomic foundations of the state. To ensure maximum protection of the proprietary system, English law has developed a formidable array of property offences aimed at protecting every conceivable interest in property. To list but some of the better known property offences, one finds: theft, numerous offences involving criminal deception and fraud; taking a motor vehicle or other conveyance without authority; abstracting electricity; blackmail; handling stolen goods; robbery; burglary; forgery; criminal damage – and so on.

The common denominator in these offences is that they involve an interference with the property interests of the victim. Both the victim himself and the community at large is harmed. The victim is deprived of his interest in property – or threatened with such deprivation. Property interests are often referred to as 'extensions of the personality'. An attack upon a victim's property interests can thus be seen as analogous to a personal attack: his 'space' has been invaded; he has been rendered impotent by the actions of a dishonest person. Insurance, like a medical operation after a physical attack, might help to 'heal the wound' but does not alter the fact that the victim has been directly harmed.

The community at large is also harmed by property offences. Apart from threatening the economic base of the social system and threatening the security interests of society, vast resources are expended on the prevention and apprehension of property offenders. Ultimately, the real cost of property crime is borne by the public or sections thereof. The cost of much shoplifting, employee theft and commercial fraud is simply passed on to the consumer. If these crimes were not committed, goods in stores could be anything up to 5 per cent cheaper than at present. Also, while insurance companies underwrite much of the economic loss in property offences, they are not charities: the real cost is borne by insured persons in increased premiums.

Despite such common features, however, each of the above listed property offences involves its own distinctive harm. What each of these harms is, and whether such features are sufficiently distinctive to justify the wide proliferation of separate offences, is the subject-matter of the remainder of this chapter.

Before starting this examination, two further points must be made. First, most of the property offences are now statutory, the Theft Act 1968 being the major statute and covering a large number of the offences. It is, however, buttressed by other legislation, notably, the Theft Act 1978, the Criminal Damage Act 1971 and the Forgery and Counterfeiting Act 1981. Much of the work here then is a matter of statutory interpretation. It is nevertheless an instructive task in helping to inform us as to how our courts have coped with an area of law beginning to approximate to a code. Such understanding is particularly important as we enter an era likely to culminate in a codification of the whole of the criminal law (Law Commission, 1985).

Secondly, the various property offences involve interference with other persons' *rights or interests in property*. It is always necessary

147

therefore to ascertain whether these other persons actually do have such rights or interests in property. The answer to such questions lies in established areas of the civil law: the law of property, contract and quasi-contract. In the leading House of Lords decision on theft, *Morris* (1984), Lord Roskill deprecated overreliance on technical civil law concepts. For instance, whether a contract is void or voidable was 'so far as possible' not a relevant question in relation to the law of theft. On one hand, this approach is to be applauded. The imposition of criminal liability with its concomitant punishment should depend on fundamental issues – such as blameworthiness and the causing of harm; it should not depend on complex, and sometimes controversial, fine points of civil law relating to the passing of property. On the other hand, however, to commit a property offence, some other person must have some legally recognised interest in that property. If no other person has any such interest in the property no crime can be committed as, generally, an owner is free to use and abuse his own property to his heart's content. Therefore, it becomes crucial to establish whether the other person does have a legal interest in the property. How can this question be answered? By the jury, on a 'common-sense' basis? Or, by judges devising new definitions of established civil law concepts to be utilised in criminal cases? Or, by ignoring Lord Roskill's exhortations and utilising the civil law? It is these questions, and the law's inability to answer them, that have been a dominant feature in the interpretation of the various property offences, to an examination of which we now turn.

2. The Main Offences

Again, space being limited, we will concentrate on a few offences, primarily that of theft. Brief consideration will then be given to the deception offences, robbery, burglary and handling stolen goods.

Dealing first with *theft*, section 1(1) of the Theft Act 1968 provides that a 'person is guilty of theft if he dishonestly appropriates property belonging to another with the intention of permanently depriving the other of it'.

The offence thus contains five elements: (i) appropriation, (ii) property, (iii) belonging to another (these three constitute the *actus reus*); (iv) dishonesty, (v) intention of permanent deprivation (these two constitute the *mens rea*). Each of these elements is defined (or sometimes merely 'illustrated'), to varying extents, by sections 2–6 of the Theft Act 1968.

Section 3(1) defines an *appropriation* as an *assumption of the rights of an owner*. It is thus necessary that the defendant treat the goods as his own: he must regard them as his to take away, use or abuse. This concept of appropriation is, however, highly ambiguous in that it could cover someone who has done nothing objectively wrong yet, but who has decided to steal the property and is secretly treating the property as his own. For instance, in *Eddy v. Niman* (1981) the defendant in a supermarket placed goods in the store's wire basket with an intention of stealing them. It could be argued that, because of this intention, he was assuming the rights of owner: he had decided not to pay for the goods; he was going to make off with them when and how he chose; he was dealing with the goods as if they were his and not the supermarket's property. It was held in this case, however, that such a secret intention of stealing was insufficient. He had not yet done anything wrong because he had only done what the store expected him to do, namely, he had simply placed the goods in the wire basket provided for exactly that purpose.

This approach was confirmed in the leading House of Lords decision in *Morris* (1984) where it was ruled that an appropriation must involve the doing of something *objectively inconsistent* with the rights of the owner. An appropriation is 'not an act expressly or impliedly authorised by the owner but an act by way of adverse interference with or usurpation of those rights'. So there would be an appropriation in a case such as *McPherson* (1973) where the defendant in a supermarket placed two bottles of whisky in her *own shopping bag* – an act she was not authorised to do. Similarly, there was an appropriation in *Morris* (1984) itself where a dishonest shopper switched the price labels on goods and then placed them in the trolley. The shopper here was doing something he was not supposed to do and assuming the rights of an owner in respect of the more expensive item – or, at any rate, he was assuming some of the rights of the owner which was held to suffice for an appropriation.

This whole approach is to be welcomed in that it is highly anomalous to suggest that a person who has not yet done anything wrong is already a thief by virtue of his criminal intentions! At such a point he has done nothing manifestly criminal; no harm has yet occurred; criminal liability at this stage would be tantamount to punishment for 'thought-crimes' – an unacceptable notion (see earlier, page 26).

Nevertheless, this approach is not without its difficulties. In the earlier House of Lords decision of *Lawrence* (1972) the defendant, a taxi driver, grossly overcharged an Italian who had just arrived in this country. The Italian, on getting into the taxi, had offered the defendant £1. The defendant, stating that this was insufficient, helped himself to a further £6 from the Italian's wallet. The Italian was holding out his wallet and thus 'consenting' to the removal of the further £6. The correct fare was approximately 10s.6d. The defendant was charged with theft of 'the approximate sum of £6'. It was held in this case that the taxi-driver appropriated the money when he took it from the wallet and that it was irrelevant whether the owner consented to his taking the property.

Such an approach appears inconsistent with *Morris* (1984). If the owner is consenting to the defendant taking his property, the defendant is hardly doing anything inconsistent with the owner's rights. However, there is one possible way of reconciling these two decisions: because of the taxi-driver's fraud in misrepresenting the cost of the journey he was in fact doing something objectively inconsistent with the Italian's rights – he was taking £6 that he was not entitled to take and to the taking of which the Italian, because of the fraud, had not truly consented. He was thus appropriating the money.

Theft is concerned with the appropriation of property, and 'property' is given a wide definition in section 4(1) so as to include 'money and all other property, real or personal, including things in action and other intangible property'. However subsections (2)–(4) of section 4 severely limit the circumstances in which land, wild plants and wild creatures may be stolen.

The property must 'belong to another'. This does not mean that the property must really belong to another in the sense that that other must *own* it. The law of theft aims to protect a wider range of interests than mere ownership and section 5 accordingly defines 'belonging to another' in a wide and, at times, an artificial manner. Property is 'regarded as' belonging to any of the following persons: (i) one who has possession or control of the property (section 5(1)); (ii) one who has any proprietary right or interest in the property (section 5(1)); this includes the obvious instance of actually owning the property; (iii) where property is subject to a trust, one who has a right to enforce the trust (section 5(2)); (iv) one who gives property to another, placing that other under a legal obligation to deal with the property or its proceeds in a particular way (section 5(3)); (v) one who parts with property by mistake in circumstances where the recipient is under a legal obligation to make restoration of the property (section 5(4)).

It is in relation to this concept of 'belonging to another' that the law has been faced with the necessity of introducing civil law concepts in deciding, for example, whether someone has a 'proprietary right or interest' in the property, or whether he is owed a 'legal obligation' by the defendant in respect of the property. For instance, in *Kaur v. Chief Constable for Hampshire* (1981) the defendant chose a pair of shoes from a rack of shoes marked at £6.99 per pair; one shoe was marked at £6.99 and the other £4.99. Without concealing either label she took the shoes to the cashier hoping to be charged the lower price – which she was. She paid the £4.99, placed the shoes in her shopping bag and left the store. She was charged with theft but her conviction was quashed on appeal. She had appropriated the shoes when, having paid for them, she placed them in her own shopping bag. But at that point she was not appropriating property 'belonging to another': the cashier had authority to charge the price specified on the shoe; the cashier's mistake in charging £4.99 was not so fundamental as to destroy the validity of the contract; the contract was *voidable*; property passes under voidable contracts. Accordingly, the defendant was appropriating property belonging to herself and hence not liable for theft.

In *Williams* (1980) the defendant, an enterprising but dishonest schoolboy, went to Stanley Gibbons and purchased some obsolete Jugoslav dinar for £7. He then went to the *bureau de change* at a department store and cashed in the obsolete dinar for some £107 – a quick £100 profit on the transaction. His conviction for theft was upheld: he had appropriated the £107 when he received it from the *bureau de change* and placed it in his pocket. The cashier had made a fundamental mistake in handing over the money; the contract was thus *void ab initio*; property never passed to the defendant who had, accordingly, appropriated property belonging to another, namely, the store.

As already mentioned, Lord Roskill in *Morris* (1984) indicated that questions of civil law, such as whether contracts are void or voidable, should not be injected into the law of theft. But if such issues are excluded, on what basis can one decide whether property does 'belong to another' in cases such as *Kaur v. Chief Constable for Hampshire* (1981) and *Williams* (1980)? As indicated earlier (page 147), the law of theft exists largely to regulate interests in property. It would be somewhat anomalous to define these interests in one manner for the purposes of the civil law – and then to ignore that definition in the criminal law – when one of the main objectives of the criminal law in this field is to safeguard and uphold these same property interests as defined in the civil law. Theft is not a 'conduct crime' dispensing with the need for a direct harm (see earlier, page 113). It is a 'result crime': there must be a direct harm of a victim being deprived of his interest in property – an interest that only exists by virtue of the civil law. It is interesting that the first reported case after *Morris* (1984) was *Walker* (1984) in which the Court of Appeal held that recourse to the civil law was 'inevitable'. To decide whether the property in that case 'belonged to another', the trial judge should have explained the Sale of Goods Act 1979 to the jury!

What is the requisite degree of blameworthiness required for theft? It has already been argued that the concept of 'blame' is broader than that of *mens rea*. *Mens rea* generally is taken to refer to intention, foresight, knowledge etc. in relation to existing circumstances or the consequences of the defendant's actions. Such a typical *mens rea* element is indeed incorporated into theft in that the defendant must intend to deprive his victim permanently of his interest in the property. But, additionally, the defendant's actions must be blameworthy in that his actions must be *dishonest*.

Dishonesty is a moral concept. The taking of property must be one to which 'moral obloquy can reasonably' be attached (*Feely*, 1973). The defendant can be fairly blamed for disregarding the value system inherent in the law of theft – a value system that underwrites the importance of preserving property rights.

But how is this requisite degree of blame, dishonesty, to be established? Section 2 of the Theft Act 1968 specifies three specific situations which do *not* amount to dishonesty, namely, where the defendant believes: (a) that he has in law the right to deprive the victim of the property; or (b) that the victim would consent to the appropriation; or (c) that the person to whom the property belongs cannot be discovered by taking reasonable steps (section 2(1)). Apart from these three cases the concept of dishonesty is left undefined in the Theft Act 1968. In *Feely* (1973) it was held that it should remain undefined and be left entirely to the jury. Whether conduct was dishonest was to be judged by the 'current standards of ordinary decent folk' – and who better to assess this than the ordinary decent folk sitting in the jury box who could simply apply their own standards to the everyday concept 'dishonesty'. The jury had to ascertain the state of the defendant's mind – for example, when he 'borrowed' the money, did he know that this was not permitted? Did he believe he could repay it soon? – and so on – and then the jury had to assess, applying their own standards of morality, whether the defendant, with his beliefs, was dishonest.

But what of the defendant whose actions might be regarded as dishonest by the jury applying their standards, but who adamantly maintains (and is believed) that according to *his* system of values, he was acting honestly? For example, in *Gilks* (1972) the defendant claimed that he thought he was honest in keeping money mistakenly paid to him by a bookmaker because he thought bookmakers were 'a race apart' and thus fair game. The courts were faced with a quandary here. Acceptance of such pleas would undercut the moral imperative laid down by the criminal law. The criminal law largely reflects (and attempts to uphold) community values. The *Feely* (1973) test allows these community values to be enunciated by a so-called representative section of the community, namely, the jury. If the values of the jury and the community are to be ignored and replaced by the values of the defendant, (who, for example, might endorse the political ideology that 'property is theft'), the result would be a complete absence of any objective standard. The door would be open to the 'Robin Hood defence'. The defendant would effectively become his own judge and jury.

On the other hand, the courts were reluctant to dismiss such pleas totally. The criminal law is based largely on the premise of moral responsibility. We blame those who are morally at fault. If a defendant openly rejects the value system inherent in the law of theft, he can be blamed even if, according to his own values, he thinks his actions are honest. He has knowingly 'declared war' on the values of society and can be blamed therefor. It can never be an excuse in the criminal law that one does not agree with any given law. But what of the defendant who genuinely thinks he is acting honestly according to his values – *and* who really believes that most other people would agree with him as to the morality of his conduct – and can convince a jury of these beliefs? Such a defendant is not openly defying the law; he believes he is upholding the value system inherent in the law of theft. The case for exempting such a defendant from blame becomes strong.

This latter thinking was endorsed in the leading decision of *Ghosh* (1982) which lays down that a defendant acts 'dishonestly' if what he does is dishonest according to the ordinary standards of reasonable and honest people (the *Feely*, 1973, test), *and* if he realised that what he was doing was dishonest according to those standards. Thus using the examples given in *Ghosh* (1982) itself: Robin Hood or anti-vivisectionists who remove animals from vivisection laboratories are acting dishonestly, even though they may consider themselves to be morally justified in so acting *provided that they know* that ordinary people would consider such actions to be dishonest.

This test has been subjected to fierce and widespread criticism along the lines that it will lead to uncertainty and inconsistency in the application of the law; it will tend to increase the number of trials and lengthen and complicate them (by defendants 'chancing their arm' and claiming they were honest); our society is no longer culturally homogeneous and therefore juries are not able clearly to reflect shared values; with the disappearance of objective standards,

'Robin Hood' and other 'odd' defendants could (just) escape liability; it could lead to inadequate protection of the property rights of 'unpopular classes of owners' – bookmakers, animal experimenters, multinational corporations, and all those from whom many persons regard theft as a 'perk' of their job.

A full response to these criticisms is beyond the scope of this book. But, as explained above, *Ghosh* (1982) is capable of defence. The quest throughout the criminal law is for the isolation of the blameworthy. If the jury, reflecting community standards, can attach 'moral obloquy' to the defendant's actions and are satisfied that the defendant knows he is acting contrary to the moral standards of ordinary people, a judgement of blameworthiness is truly appropriate. The test has tried to combine the need to preserve objective standards within the criminal law with the need to maintain the importance of moral fault (Wasik, 1979). Some of the edges of the *Ghosh* (1982) test are rough – but one does not cut down an entire tree because of some dead twigs!

Finally, it must be established that the defendant intended *permanently* to deprive the victim of his interest (whether possession or ownership or whatever) in the property. The criminal law is generally not concerned with temporary deprivations of property, no matter how dishonest. (There are two exceptions here when temporary removals will be criminal: removal of articles from places open to the public (Theft Act 1968, section 11) and taking a motor vehicle or other conveyance without authority (Theft Act 1968, section 12)).

In England there is no full definition of 'intention of permanently depriving' but section 6 provides 'illustrations' of the concept (*Warner*, 1970) and specifies, among other things, that a borrowing or a lending may be theft if 'for a period and in circumstances making it equivalent to an outright taking or disposal' (section 6(1)). In *Lloyd, Bhuee and Ali* (1985) it was held that this only applied where there was an intention to return the 'thing' in such a changed state that effectively 'all its goodness or virtue' had gone. For example, if one 'borrowed' a football season ticket and returned the piece of paper at the end of the season, 'all its goodness or virtue' would have been destroyed. But if, as in *Lloyd, Bhuee and Ali* (1985), films are taken from a cinema, copied for the purpose of producing private videotapes and then returned to the cinema, such films would not have lost 'their virtue' and therefore there would be no liability for theft in such a case.

The remaining property offences selected for discussion here can be dealt with more briefly. There are several offences relating to criminal *deception*, each offence specifying a different commodity that is dishonestly obtained by the deception, most notably (i) property (Theft Act 1968, section 15), (ii) pecuniary advantage (Theft Act 1968, section 16(2)(b) and (c)), (iii) services (Theft Act 1978, section 1), (iv) evasion of liability (Theft Act 1978, section 2).

The common feature of the deception offences is that a 'deception' must have taken place and this deception must have *caused* the defendant to obtain the specified commodity. The courts, however, have adopted a somewhat cavalier approach towards the necessity for establishing legal causation. Wanting to punish the blameworthy (dishonest practisers of deceptions), they have seemingly been content to adopt the approach (criticised earlier, page 101) that if blame is established, along with 'but for' causation, then the result cannot be too remote and legal causation can be deemed to be established (earlier, page 102). For instance, in *Lambie* (1982) the defendant purchased goods from Mothercare and paid by Barclaycard, knowing she was way beyond her credit limit and that Barclays were trying to contact her. The assistant accepted the payment by Barclaycard after checking that the defendant's name was not on the current 'stop-list'. The House of Lords upheld the defendant's original conviction despite the fact that the assistant had made it clear that she was not interested in the state of the customer's credit. Having checked the 'stop-list' and Lambie's signature, she knew that payment was guaranteed by Barclays; that is the whole point of credit cards; she did not care about the relationship between Barclays and the customer. It thus seems somewhat contrived to assert that the assistant was deceived and as a result of that deception was induced to enter into the contract with Lambie. Yet that was precisely what the House of Lords held. Presenting the Barclaycard was an implied representation that the defendant had authority from her bank to enter into a contract (as agent for the bank) with the shop:

this representation was untrue and thus constituted a deception; this deception was the effective cause of the assistant agreeing to contract with Lambie because *if she had known* that Lambie was acting dishonestly and with no authority to use the card, she would not have entered into the contract. Such reasoning is only explicable on the basis that the House of Lords, concerned by the increasing potential for credit card frauds, was determined to convict a blameworthy credit card-holder – even at the cost of having to deem the victim to have been deceived and thereby induced into accepting a credit card.

A related offence, but one that does not require any deception, is created by section 3 of the Theft Act 1978, namely, dishonestly *making off without payment* when payment is expected 'on the spot' (for example, running out of a restaurant without paying).

The crime of *robbery*, contrary to section 8 of the Theft Act 1968, is committed if a person uses force or threatens force in order to steal. There must be a theft and thus any defence to theft will be a defence to robbery. It would appear that any degree of force or threatened force will suffice. In *Dawson* (1976) it was held that a nudge causing the victim to lose his balance was sufficient force; like 'dishonesty', 'force' is an ordinary word which can be left to juries to interpret as they see fit.

The crime of *burglary*, contrary to section 9 of the Theft Act 1968, is committed if a person enters a building as a trespasser with the intention of stealing, inflicting grievous bodily harm, raping any woman or of doing unlawful damage therein (section 9(1)(a)). (Section 9(1)(b) creates a separate species of burglary where a defendant *has entered* a building as a trespasser and then steals or attempts to steal therein, or inflicts or attempts to inflict grievous bodily harm on any person therein.) And the more serious crime of *aggravated burglary* is committed if, at the time of the burglary, the defendant has with him any firearm, offensive weapon or explosive.

The crime of burglary is well illustrated by the famous case of *Collins* (1973) – a case much loved by lawyers and students for the sheer absurdity of its factual setting and the almost unrealistic logicality of its reasoning. The defendant, Collins, was a young man who, feeling particularly lustful one night, went to the house of a girl he knew, determined to have sexual intercourse with her 'by force if necessary'. He found a stepladder, climbed up and looked into the girl's bedroom. The girl was naked and asleep. Collins descended the ladder and stripped off all his clothes with the exception of his socks. (He claimed that a more rapid escape could be effected in socks. Edmund Davies LJ found himself unable to express any view on this point!) He then climbed the ladder again and pulled himself on to the window sill with its lattice-type window. He was starting to pull himself in when the girl awoke. The girl saw a blond young male with an erect penis crouched in the open window and assumed it was her boyfriend paying her an ardent nocturnal visit! She pulled him into the room and they had sexual intercourse. However, the length of his hair(!) and his voice as they exchanged 'love talk' led her to the conclusion that 'somehow there was something different'. She turned on the light, saw that her companion was not her boyfriend, slapped and bit him and then went to the bathroom.

The defendant was charged with burglary on the basis that he had entered a building as a trespasser with the intention of raping the girl. A trespasser is one who enters without consent. If Collins had entered the room prior to the girl inviting him in, he would have been guilty of burglary as he would have entered as a trespasser, at that stage with the intention of raping her. But if, when she invited him in, he was still on the outside of the window sill, then when he did enter the building he would not have been entering as a trespasser and therefore could not be liable. The facts were not clear: he was on the window sill; while parts of his body might have been protruding into the room prior to her invitation, the Court of Appeal held that to be liable he needed to have made 'an effective and substantial entry' into the bedroom as a trespasser. As the jury had not been invited to consider this issue squarely, the conviction was quashed as being unsafe. Thus the criminal liability of Collins was made to depend entirely upon the point 'as narrow maybe as the window sill' (*Collins*, 1973) of how much of his body had entered the room at the stage she invited him in!

Finally, the crime of *handling stolen goods*, contrary to section 22 of the Theft Act 1968, is committed when a person (otherwise than in the course of stealing), knowing or believing the goods to be stolen, dishonestly receives the goods or dishonestly undertakes or assists in their retention, removal, disposal or realisation by or for the benefit of another person, or if he arranges to do so.

This offence is extremely wide. One of the most effective ways of combating theft and burglary is to make it difficult and less profitable for thieves and burglars to dispose of the goods they have stolen. Accordingly, to assist in law enforcement in this regard, section 22 casts a wide net over all persons in almost any way associated with dealing with stolen goods. It is interesting to note that one commits the offence simply by *arranging* to handle stolen goods; this is wide enough to cover persons who, without this provision, would not have done enough to be liable even for an attempt. The defendant must of course be blameworthy. His actions must be dishonest and he must know or believe that the goods are stolen: a mere suspicion is not enough – he must actually believe the goods to be stolen.

At the time of the handling the goods must still be 'stolen'. Section 24(4) is important in this regard in providing that goods cease to be stolen if they are restored to lawful possession which covers cases where the police recover stolen property. This means that if stolen goods are seized by the police who, then acting as 'undercover agents' or simple 'lookouts', attempt to apprehend receivers of the goods, conviction will be impossible as those receivers will not be handling 'stolen' goods – unless it can be established that at some earlier stage when they were still stolen the receivers *arranged* to handle the stolen goods.

3. Conclusion

We have seen that property offences are mainly concerned with the protection of a variety of interests in property. It is this interference (actual or, sometimes, simply threatened) with property interests that constitutes the primary harm in such offences. While it might be important at the sentencing stage, English law does not concern itself *at the substantive level* with the *value* of the property interest interfered with. For instance, it is as much theft to steal a can of beans as to steal £10 million. This can be contrasted with the position in the United States where, in many states, theft offences are graded according to the value of the property stolen. For instance, the Model Penal Code says that theft of property worth less than $50 constitutes a petty misdemeanour; theft of property valued at between $50 and $500 constitutes a misdemeanour; theft of property with a value exceeding $500 constitutes a felony of the third degree (section 223.1(2): there are certain qualifications to this broad structure). Each of these offence categories carries its own range of penalties.

The argument in support of the English approach is that the value of the property is only one way of assessing the extent of the harm and it cannot be made decisive. For instance, the following could be cited as possible indicators of the gravity of an offence: the characteristics of the offender (e.g. theft by a person in a position of trust); the characteristics of the victim (e.g. theft from the old or disabled; theft from individuals as opposed to theft from companies); the circumstances of the offence (e.g. pickpocketing – an 'offensive and frightening type of theft'; thefts committed jointly with others); and the non-monetary value of the goods (e.g. a key to be used subsequently for a more serious offence; property of purely sentimental value to the victim) (James Committee, 1975). There are also problems relating to the blameworthiness of the defendant. What if the pickpocket, hoping to find a few pounds, snatches a wallet containing £1000?

Despite these objections, it is submitted that property offences could be broadly subdivided so as to separate offences involving minor interferences (in terms of value) with property from the more serious cases. It seems ludicrous that theft of a can of beans or theft by an employee of a box of paperclips should be placed in the same category as major thefts and frauds involving thousands of pounds. The James Committee (1975) proposed a general £20 monetary limit, beneath which Crown Court trial would be unavailable. Section 22 of the Magistrates' Courts Act 1980 provides that various offences under the Criminal Damage Act 1971 shall be triable summarily if the value of the property does not exceed £400. It would appear to make good sense to extend such a provision beyond the confines of procedural law and into the substantive law itself.

English law, in developing the relationship of the various offences to each other and their relative levels of seriousness, has rejected such an approach and looked beyond these primary proprietary harms to the secondary consequences involved. Offences have been viewed as threats to the value system inherent in our whole concept of property. It has been 'secondary harms', much influenced by the method of committing the crime, and law enforcement considerations that have been most important in informing the present structure of property offences.

Robbery, for instance, carries a maximum penalty of life imprisonment compared to the ten-year maximum available for theft. The reasons for this are fairly self-evident, both the levels of harm and blame being aggravated. Robbery causes fear and apprehension to the victim. The robber is prepared openly to confront his victim and commit his crime in defiance of that victim. It is almost impossible to protect oneself in advance against robbers threatening violence. While recognising the force of these views, one is nevertheless forced to ask the same question, even at the danger of becoming repetitious: does the robber who pushes his victim and snatches 10p deserve to be in the same category of offence, both in terms of moral gravity and for sentencing purposes, as the robber armed with a sawn-off shotgun who holds up a security van and makes off with £100,000?

Burglary, with its maximum penalty of fourteen years' imprisonment, and aggravated burglary, carrying a maximum penalty of life imprisonment, are explicable on similar grounds. While liability for these offences need not involve any actual loss of property, the fact is that the security and sanctity of the home (in many cases) has been violated. This can cause special psychological harm: distress, alarm and the fear of knowing one is not safe even in one's own home. The lives of a large majority of victims of burglary are affected for some weeks after the burglary, and over a quarter of such victims suffer serious shock (Maguire, 1980). These harms are increased when the burglar is armed with an offensive weapon. Again, of course, if one were structuring property offences more precisely, one might here wish to draw distinctions between burglary of residential and commercial property, occupied and non-occupied buildings, and so on.

Theft and handling stolen goods are closely related offences with a considerable overlap between them. In most cases a person who handles stolen goods is 'assuming the rights of owner' over the property and is thereby appropriating it, becoming guilty of theft – assuming the other elements of the offence to be present, as they usually will be. (One cannot, however, be convicted of both theft and handling – *Shelton*, 1986.) There are, however, good reasons for retaining handling stolen goods as a distinct form of wrong-doing and not merging it within the offence of theft. First, not every case of handling will amount to theft (for example: 'arranging' to deal with the stolen goods might not involve any appropriation of the property; handling also extends to goods obtained by fraud or blackmail). Secondly, criminal offences should accurately describe the prohibited conduct as far as possible. The public perceives a clear distinction between a thief and a handler of stolen property; the law should reflect such understanding. And thirdly, it has been considered necessary to demarcate handling as a special offence subject to a maximum of fourteen years' imprisonment (as opposed to ten years for theft) for frankly utilitarian reasons. Handlers of stolen goods provide much of the market for theft; their activities are a significant source of the economic motivation behind much theft. If the law could stamp out 'fences' (professional handlers) and other handlers, much of the war against theft and burglary would have been won.

Despite these views and the potential for a higher sentence, most people today regard handling as a lesser offence in terms of moral stigma; defendants will often plead guilty to handling on condition that all charges of theft are dropped. This attitude has come about because of a growing view that handlers and purchasers of stolen goods are 'only slightly dishonest people' (Spencer, 1985) who are not as blameworthy as those who actually steal or burgle. Theft and burglary create an immediate sense of danger in the community; there must often be a risk of violence with such activities; the thief or burglar is the primary cause of harm, directly invading the rights of the owner of property. In contrast, the criminal receiver, the 'fence', is regarded only as a shady, somewhat disreputable character – and the secondary purchaser as simply someone who has succumbed to the 'natural temptation' of buying something very cheap.

The law is accordingly faced with a dilemma. On the one hand, it recognises that the punishment of handlers is crucial if theft and burglary is to be reduced but, on the other hand, it is faced by an apathetic public almost prepared to 'turn a blind eye' to handling. A possible way out of this dilemma could be to divide the offence of handling stolen goods into degrees. The more serious offence could be reserved for the professional 'fence', the lesser offence covering secondary purchasers. Such a division might be a fairer reflection of the moral stigma felt by most to attach to the two categories of handlers and could have the advantage of underwriting the necessity of enforcement against, and harm caused by, the professional handler. The danger with such an approach, however, could be that even less moral stigma would be attached to secondary purchasers than at present and, after all, it is these purchasers who buy stolen goods from fences who are the 'key element in the incentive structure that supports property crime' (*Yale Law Journal*, 1980).

The various offences of deception are, if anything, even more closely related to, and overlap with, theft. The defendants in the earlier discussed theft cases of *Lawrence* (1972), *Morris* (1984), *Williams* (1980) and perhaps *Kaur v. Chief Constable for Hampshire* (1981) could all have been charged with obtaining property by deception contrary to section 15 of the Theft Act 1968. It could thus be argued that one single broad offence such as theft could be made to embrace all 'involuntary' transfers of property, thus rendering an offence such as section 15 otiose. Such a single offence would eliminate the necessity in many cases to draw fine distinctions between closely related forms of misconduct. It could also be argued that prevailing moral standards do not differentiate sharply between the 'swindler' and the 'thief' (Model Penal Code, 1953).

On the other hand, it is submitted that English law is wise to separate theft from obtaining property by deception contrary to section 15, even though both offences carry the same maximum penalty of ten years' imprisonment. An important moral distinction exists between the two offences in the paradigmatic instances of each (even if not in some of the overlap cases). A typical theft involves a surreptitious taking; the owner is totally helpless against such a taking; if the thief is interrupted there is a risk of violence; because of his anonymity there is extra difficulty in identifying and apprehending the thief. With the typical obtaining property by deception, however, the victim has also 'lost' his property – but he handed it over 'voluntarily'; he had an opportunity to resist – with greater alertness he might not have been deceived; the deceiver has not resorted to stealth or force and often will have had to face his victim openly, thereby increasing the chances of subsequent identification and apprehension. While some of these differences might suggest that section 15 ought to carry a lesser potential punishment than theft, the fact remains that the 'big-time con-man' can inflict massive losses upon large numbers of persons simultaneously and so the high maximum penalty is perhaps necessary to cover such cases.

Also revealing is the variety of penalties available for the different deception offences. While section 15 carries a ten-year maximum penalty, section 16 (obtaining a pecuniary advantage by deception – for example, obtaining an overdraft or employment by deception) carries a maximum penalty of five years' imprisonment. Obtaining services by deception and evasion of liability by deception, contrary to sections 1 and 2 of the Theft Act 1978 respectively, also carry a five-year maximum penalty. On the other hand, making off without payment contrary to section 3 of the Theft Act 1978 only carries a maximum penalty of two years' imprisonment. This last offence is the only one on this list that does not necessitate proof of a deception; it is thus in some ways more akin to theft in that the participation of the victim is not necessary for the commission of the offence. With regard to this offence it seems likely that the lesser penalty is linked to the economic loss sustained by the victim. Under section 3 one is dealing primarily with persons who rush out of restaurants, petrol stations or hotels without paying. While, admittedly, bills in certain London restaurants and hotels can be astronomic, they will never be of such a magnitude as to warrant imprisonment for more than two years. On the other hand, the economic loss occasioned by theft and the deception offences can be huge, running into millions of pounds, in which case a higher penalty could be seen as appropriate. Such reasoning, however, does not explain the differential in sentences available for section 15 and the other deception offences.

With all these offences, and indeed all those discussed in this book, it is submitted that a more coherent structure is needed which must be related to some clear principle and policy. It is simply not good enough to proceed on the present rather *ad hoc* basis. As suggested earlier (page 123), the way forward is to structure *all* offences by combining the degree of harm caused with the degree of blameworthiness involved. In this way the relative seriousness of offences can be fixed. It is only with such a clearly structured substantive law that the criminal law can seriously attempt to perform its true function in our society. It is to an examination of this function that we now turn.

4

The Function of Law in Society

A. INTRODUCTION

All law, including the criminal law, is designed as a mechanism for achieving social control. Its purpose is the regulation of conduct and activities within society. The criminal law, however, differs from other branches of law in that it employs *stigmatic punishment* against those who violate its commands. It attempts to reflect those fundamental social values expressing the way we live and then uses this 'big stick' of punishment as a means of reinforcing those values and securing compliance therewith. In this way it seeks to protect not only the individual, but also the very structure and fabric of society.

From this it can be seen that the function of the criminal law is threefold:

1. Initially, it must identify which conduct should be brought within its ambit. If all law is designed as a means of social control, on what basis is the decision made to *criminalise* conduct, as opposed to leaving it to regulation by other, less harsh, areas of law?

2. Having decided on the values needing protection through the 'blunt instrument' of the criminal law, the function of the criminal law becomes one of upholding these values and thereby, and in other ways, of reducing crime.

The achievement of such goals presupposes a certain degree of actual enforcement of the criminal law: a law that was never enforced would soon become a dead letter.

3. Given these objectives, the final function of the criminal law is one of isolating *who* should be punished and *how much* punishment is appropriate. In fulfilling this final function, the criminal law is presently having to face a critical challenge. If the main task of the

criminal law is crime prevention, must decisions as to who to punish and how to punish be made from a crime prevention perspective? For instance, life imprisonment for parking offences would probably greatly reduce the incidence of such offences, if not totally eliminate them. On the other hand, while possibly effective, such a punishment would be totally *undeserved* and *unjust*. In its role of distributing and measuring punishment, and conversely of structuring criminal offences, the function of the criminal law is one of pinpointing those who *deserve* punishment and for whom punishment would be *just* – and of grading the severity of their punishment according to such criteria.

It is to an examination of these functions that we now turn.

B. CRIMINALISING CONDUCT

One does not use a sledgehammer to crack a nut. One should not use the criminal law to control conduct that can be effectively regulated by other areas of law. For instance, it was argued earlier, in relation to strict liability offences (page 98), that much prohibited conduct could be decriminalised and made subject to regulation by administrative action and remedies. In any society that values liberty, the criminal law ought only to be invoked as a last-resort method of social control when absolutely necessary.

But when is it *necessary* to criminalise conduct? How does one decide whether certain conduct should be prohibited by the criminal law or not? Clearly, particular decisions need reference to the social, economic and psychological realities surrounding a given activity. But are there any underlying principles that can guide and influence such decisions? If one were trying to determine whether consensual buggery, possession of narcotic drugs or trespass ought to be criminal, how and on what basis would the decision be made?

Discussion here will start with a brief summary of two highly controversial schools of thought before proceeding to the more familiar territory in which this debate is generally waged.

First, there are the views of a school of thought loosely described as 'radical criminology'. The criminal law represents nothing more than the vested interests of the powerful. It is an expression of power by an elite which is used as a prop to maintain the present social, economic and class structure. In short, it 'keeps the lid on the lower classes' (Carlen, 1980). Only conduct affecting interests regarded as significant by this power-group is criminalised.

Such views are particularly important in understanding the phenomenon of crime (who commits crimes and why) and the enforcement of the criminal law: for example, why social security frauds are prosecuted to a much greater extent than tax frauds. And, indeed, many offences are explicable in terms of such a theory, for example, property offences and the new public order offences created in the wake of violence during the 1984/5 miners' strike.

The problem with radical criminology as an explanation of criminalisation, however, is its failure to explain how we identify which interests are sufficiently important to the power-group to warrant criminalisation. Particularly when moving away from economic crimes, how does one identify the vested interests of the power-group? Which of their interests are being challenged by victimless crime? With such crimes, ultimately, the interests of this group are largely synonymous with the interests of most persons in society. For instance, it is difficult to see how adult homosexuality or sado-masochistic beatings threaten the interests of the power-group in society any more than they threaten the interests of all persons – and to say that an activity is made criminal when it threatens the interests of society is simply not helpful as the very problem under consideration is one of identifying *when* conduct *sufficiently* threatens society to *justify* criminalising it. In other words, with too many of the really controversial issues, radical criminology can provide no real independent explanation and one is forced to try and find answers according to the general criteria shortly to be considered.

The second controversial new school of thought is that which endorses an economic theory of the criminal law. This theory has mostly been directed at the individual's decision to commit a crime and at the economics of law enforcement and deterrent punishment. More recently, however, attempts have been made to subject the substantive criminal law and issues of criminalisation to an economic analysis.

The Function of Law in Society

The object of the criminal law is to discourage 'market bypassing', thereby promoting 'economically efficient' acts. The market is the most efficient method of allocating resources. Such efficiency must be promoted by discouraging people from bypassing the market. Putting it another way, an individual should not be allowed to seize for himself something that he could have bargained for. Conduct is criminalised so that the criminal sanction can operate to induce market behaviour. For example, it is more efficient to force me to buy a car than to allow me to steal it; by stealing, I am taking something that I could have bargained for. This is the rationale of theft and other acquisitive crimes.

Even more controversial is the economic analysis explaining why crimes of passion and violence such as murder and rape are criminalised. Posner (1985) suggests several reasons relating to the inefficiency of such actions which involve a bypassing of the market. Markets can be explicit or implicit. In a 'market' people are compensated for parting with things of value to them. A mugger is bypassing an explicit market: he is deriving satisfaction in a manner that confers no benefit on other people and is obtaining an advantage he has not bargained for. There are also implicit markets – for example, in friendship, love and respect. By raping a woman instead of securing her consent to intercourse, the rapist is bypassing such an implicit market in sex/friendship/love.

While economics might be useful in contributing to our understanding of criminal behaviour, optimal enforcement policy and deterrent punishment, its utility for our present purpose is limited. Surely, a deliberate breach of contract is 'bypassing the market'. From an economic perspective, it is difficult to see any distinction between such conduct and theft (Schulhoffer, 1985) – yet nobody seriously advances a claim that all deliberate breaches of contract should be criminalised. Similarly, many torts involve seizing entitlements that could have been bargained for. The economic theory does not help elucidate the distinction between tort and crime. Nor does the theory explain victimless crimes. Trading in narcotic drugs clearly involves bargaining for a voluntary transfer of the drugs. Such activity is economically efficient and its criminalisation cannot be justified in economic terms. Is prostitution or consensual sadomasochism bypassing an implicit market in love and marriage when both parties have chosen to reject such a market?

This economic theory is plainly flawed by its failure to recognise the moral content of the criminal law – the moral assessment of harm and blameworthy conduct (involving notions of responsibility). Economic theory focuses exclusively on the inducement aspect of the criminal law (deterrence). No mention is made of desert and justice. To that extent the analysis fails to deal with the reality of the criminal law. It paints a black and white picture of an area of law notorious for its bright colouring.

Most theorists in this field do recognise the importance of the moral content of the criminal law. One of the central burning issues, however, is whether it is justifiable to use the criminal law purely to enforce moral standards. For example, if homosexual activity, albeit consensual, were regarded as immoral, would that be a good enough reason, in itself, for criminalising it? Was President Nixon (1970) justified in supporting strict obscenity laws on the ground that 'the pollution of our civilisation with smut and filth is as serious a situation . . . as the pollution of our once pure air and water. . . . American morality is not to be trifled with'?

Lord Devlin (1959) has argued that a common morality is essential for the preservation of any society. If the moral bonds holding it together are loosened, society will disintegrate. Accordingly, as society must protect itself, it is entitled to legislate against immorality. However, while *entitled* to do so, there are certain 'practical' limits; most notably, there must be toleration of a maximum amount of individual freedom consistent with the integrity of society. But when the 'limits of tolerance' have been passed, conduct must be criminalised. Thus a grey area exists where, in the interests of freedom, immoral conduct will be permitted – but when the limits of moral intolerance are passed (the cacophony of 'intolerance, indignation, and disgust'), the conduct in question must be made criminal.

Such 'legal moralism' is rejected by the liberal school of thought, the forefather of which, John Stuart Mill (1859), boldly claimed that 'the only purpose for which power can be rightfully exercised over any member of a civilised community, against his will, is *to prevent harm to others'*. A century later the Wolfenden Committee (1957) expressed a similar view that 'there must remain a realm of private morality and immorality which is, in brief and crude terms, not the law's business.'

Such a 'do your own thing as long as you don't hurt anyone else' philosophy is naturally attractive (at least to anyone of the slightest liberal persuasion), but the approach is in fact unhelpful unless one has a clear definition of the inherently ambiguous concept 'harm to others'. For instance, the taking of narcotic drugs causes no *direct* harm to others but the drug-user might become addicted to drugs and unable to maintain his family; arguably, society is 'harmed' by having to provide support for such persons. Do such 'secondary harms' to others justify the imposition of criminal liability? And what of 'harms' that have been consented to? Is a person harmed by a sado-masochistic flogging that he requested, or by euthanasia? And how does the harm principle account for the non-criminal classification of deliberate but legitimate business competition which results in bankruptcy and ruin for the unsuccessful competitor, or abandoning one's wife and children? Further, it is possible to expand one's definition of harm. Gross (1979) defines 'harm' as the violation of the interests of another. One has an interest in avoiding unpleasant experiences. Are you then 'harmed' if the man sitting opposite you in the train begins to masturbate or to defecate or is wearing a T-shirt bearing an offensive racist slogan? And, finally, as members of society, we are arguably 'harmed' by threats upon the structure and foundations of that society. Following Lord Devlin, could one actually be 'harmed' by threats upon the common morality?

Problems such as these make it obvious that a simple 'harm to others' principle is inadequate unless one's concept of 'harm' is closely defined, and even then, some further supplementary criteria might be needed before the criminalisation of conduct can be justified.

One of the most ambitious attempts at such a careful refinement of the harm concept is that of Feinberg (1984) who argues that criminalisation is only justified if it would be effective in preventing or reducing harm to other persons or if it were necessary to prevent serious offence to other persons. 'Harm' is defined for these purposes as a 'thwarting, setting back, or defeating of an interest' that is a consequence of a *wrongful* act or omission by another. The assessment of whether an act is 'wrongful' or not is made largely on the basis of moral judgments. For instance, justified or excused conduct is not wrongful. Thus, according to this view, if the victim consents to the risks or injuries he has not been 'wronged' and so not 'harmed'. Again, the legitimate businessman has not 'wronged' his competitor and thus cannot have 'harmed' him.

Feinberg (1985) also argues that one is justified in criminalising conduct if it would probably be an effective way of preventing serious offence (and if no other means, such as the civil law, would be equally effective). Again, the criminal law can only be concerned with *wrongful* offence. Recognising that offence is less serious than harm (and so, at most, should only attract light penalties), criminalisation can be justified only if the offence caused is *serious* (defined by reference to the extent and duration of the repugnance), whether it could be reasonably avoided and whether the victim assumed the risk of being offended *and* if these factors are not counterbalanced by the *reasonableness* of the offending party's conduct (measured by the personal importance of the conduct to the actor, its general social value, the availability of alternative times and places where the conduct would cause less offence, and the extent to which the offence is caused by spiteful motives). Applying these tests to one of Feinberg's own examples, public coprophagia (public eating of faeces) in front of a captive audience (on a moving bus): the conduct causes serious offence; this is not counterbalanced by independent reasonableness. Criminalisation could be justified *if* that were assessed to be an *effective* and *necessary* means of combating such conduct.

These two criteria, harm and serious offence, are, to Feinberg, the *only* grounds for justifiable criminalisation. He rejects 'legal paternalism' (preventing people from harming themselves), legal moralism (preventing inherently immoral conduct) and the idea of punishing on the basis of other 'free-floating' secondary harms.

This debate, as to whether the criminal law should be utilised to enforce morality or to prevent harm (or deep offence) to others, does not purport to resolve fully the issue as to which conduct should be criminalised. Most commentators would insist that further conditions be satisfied before use of the criminal law is justified. In other words, the fact that conduct is highly immoral or causes harm to others (or is deeply offensive) is a *minimal condition*. Without this first hurdle being overcome, criminal liability can never be justified. But it is not a sufficient condition. Further hurdles must be overcome to establish that use of the criminal law is *necessary* and *profitable*.

In the interests of liberty all law has to pass the *test of necessity*. Is a law necessary to prevent or control an activity? Other non-legal means of social control should be employed if possible. For instance, education and advertising are, in the interests of freedom, a preferred method of trying to reduce the smoking of cigarettes in our society. Further, if some form of legal control is to be employed it should be both necessary and profitable to employ the *criminal* law – as opposed to non-criminal methods of legal regulation such as tort law, licensing and other administrative law. Overutilisation of the criminal law will lead to a devaluation of its currency.

The use of the criminal law must be *profitable* in the sense that the gains derived from its use outweigh any associated losses. Put another way, the benefits of criminalising conduct must outweigh the costs. What are these 'benefits' and 'costs' and how are they measured?

The 'gains' or 'benefits' sought by the criminal law are easily stated, namely, the prevention or reduction of crime. An evaluation of this aim of the criminal law and the difficulty of measuring it forms the main body of the remaining sections of this book. Suffice it to provide here one simple illustration of what is meant by 'gains' in this respect. If the law makes failing to wear a seat-belt an offence, then there is a 'gain' if most people do in fact wear a seat-belt. Indeed, there is a 'gain' if more people wear a seat-belt than before the enactment of that law. However, it is more difficult to establish that this 'gain' was secured *by* the criminal law; other factors, such as education by advertising, might have been highly instrumental in securing the 'gain'. On the other hand, it is clear that little 'gain' can be derived from the invocation of a criminal law that cannot be effective. For instance, a law punishing vomiting in public could have no 'gain' as, in most cases, vomiting is an involuntary action whose occurrence could not be affected by any law.

'Costs' can be assessed in both economic and non-economic terms. Economically, the costs of any criminal law will depend very largely on the level of enforcement of that law – the costs of preventative action, detection, prosecution and punishment of violators. An assessment of such costing depends, of course, upon the individual crime and the type of preventative or detective measures required, the police manpower involved, and actual extent of enforcement of the law. There is however immense difficulty in measuring the costs of any one law or, more importantly, trying to estimate what costs would be saved if a particular crime were decriminalised. For instance, if the offence of gross indecency between men, contrary to section 13 of the Sexual Offences Act 1956, and related offences were decriminalised, the police would presumably cease the expensive practice of 'staking out' public lavatories in order to apprehend criminals. However, the amount of money allocated to police departments is not dependent upon the number of offences on the statute book. Resources saved by the decriminalisation of one offence would be spent on other offences, pushing up their 'costs'.

The non-economic costs of the criminal law are significant and varied. In the famous words of Jeremy Bentham (1789), 'All punishment is mischief: all punishment in itself is evil.' Bentham was here referring to a variety of evils: the evil of having liberty restricted (felt by those obeying the law); the evil of fearing punishment and then actually suffering that punishment (felt by those breaking the law); and derivative evils such as the pain of sympathy (felt by those connected to the criminal, such as family). Naturally, the effect on the individual here varies from crime to crime and among individuals. With some crimes – say, buggery with animals – the costs in terms of stigmatisation are immense. Conviction for such an offence can spell ruin for the offender.

Another 'cost' to be added to the list is the potential 'criminogenic effect' of the criminal law. Put simply, this means that crime can breed crime. This can occur in two ways. First, under the 'labelling theory' once a person is labelled 'a criminal' he will start acting in comformity with that label and will be more easily tempted to commit further crimes. This potential 'cost' must clearly be borne in mind before criminalising conduct, especially minor crimes; once labelled a criminal it is a short step from minor to major crime. Secondly, crime can breed crime by creating an environment or circumstances in which the commission of other crimes becomes highly likely. For instance, the existence of drug offences greatly increases the cost of drugs to consumers. An addict will thus often have to commit other crimes, such as theft, in order to feed his dependency. This can lead to association with other criminals, again increasing the likelihood of yet further crime.

Outlawing certain activities, for example drug-trafficking and peddling pornography, leads to the creation of illicit black markets whose products are uncontrolled and untaxed and which create ideal economic conditions for organised crime to operate. The decriminalisation of such activities renders them more easily capable of regulation. Abortion is a good example here. Since the Abortion Act 1967 abortion has been legal in a fairly wide range of circumstances. This has resulted in a 'squeezing out' of 'back-street abortionists' with resultant higher standards of regulation and safety as abortions are increasingly performed by qualified personnel in properly equipped hospitals.

If an activity is made criminal, that law needs to be enforced, at least to some extent. A total lack of enforcement contradicts the moral message communicated by the law and raises 'the spectacle of nullification of the legislature's solemn commands' and can breed an attitude of cynicism towards the law (Kadish, 1967). But the 'costs' of such enforcement can be great – particularly in relation to certain crimes. Some laws, particularly those involving consensual sexual activities, can only be enforced in a degrading manner usually involving an unacceptable invasion of privacy. When the only way to enforce the law is for policemen to conceal themselves in the ceilings of public lavatories watching the activities below through peepholes, one must surely scrutinise the gains from such debasing conduct most carefully before concluding that they outweigh such a corrupting cost.

Other laws, particularly 'street crimes', raise the danger of discriminatory enforcement. This was an important reason behind the abolition of the old 'sus' law (Vagrancy Act 1824, sections 4, 6.) which made it an offence for a 'suspected person or reputed thief' to frequent or loiter in a public place with intent to commit an arrestable offence. One could only be a 'suspected person' in the mind of a policeman – thus presenting alarming scope for discriminatory law enforcement (Demuth, 1978).

Of course, in weighing these costs and benefits several crucial issues must be taken into account such as the magnitude and probability of the harm (or offence or deviation from the moral code if espousing legal moralism). Naturally, the greater the harm and the more likely its occurrence, the less will be the significance attached to the 'costs' of such a crime. For instance, the costs of enforcing a law prohibiting the sexual abuse of small children might be high, but the harm involved is so great that the gains to be derived from such a law clearly outweigh such costs. Also important is the social utility and degree of acceptance of the conduct in question. The greater the social utility (for example, the value attached to speedy public transport) and acceptability of the conduct (for example, alcohol consumption), the greater must be the harm and the gains to be derived before criminalisation is justified.

As the above analysis clearly reveals, there is no simple answer to determine exactly what conduct ought to be criminalised. There are competing guiding principles and a bewildering array of qualifying conditions. Suffice it to conclude by repeating two points central to the philosophy of this book. The criminal law should never be invoked unless there is no other way of dealing with the problem. Secondly, the criminal law has a clear moral content (which should preferably be expressed in a moral definition of 'harm'). While the decision to criminalise must be subject to rigorous scrutiny to ensure that such a law could be effective and that the gains would outweigh the costs, nevertheless, moral values will ultimately tip the scales in any close decision. It is these moral values that inform our distinction between various offences, such as murder and manslaughter. It would indeed be an odd system of criminal law that allowed its basic structure to be governed by moral values yet denied such values a decisive role in the anterior, but fundamental, question of what conduct should be criminalised in the first place.

C. CRIME REDUCTION

Criminalisation is concerned with identifying those values so important to society as to need enshrining in the criminal law. Once that decision has been made, the function of the criminal law becomes one of maintaining, and securing maximum compliance with, those values. When the values are maintained, most people do not contemplate crime. For the remainder, the criminal law uses stigmatic punishment as a mechanism for preventing or minimising the incidence of criminal activity. Either way, the net aim is one of securing a reduction of crime.

1 Maintaining Values

All laws have a symbolic or expressive function. We have laws against race and sex discrimination – not purely to provide a remedy for the victims of such discrimination, but also to convey and underline the important message that such discrimination is *wrong*. Expressing this message through the *criminal* law, with its potential stigmatic consequences, emphasises the total rejection of the activity in question. (For this reason it can be argued that certain instances of direct discrimination *should* have been criminalised to make the message 'stronger'.)

Simply declaring an activity to be criminal can, in itself, have a symbolic effect in influencing attitudes and moral beliefs. This point is illustrated by the research of Kaufmann (1970) who asked a group of subjects to evaluate the morality of certain behaviour (failing to rescue a drowning man). Some subjects were told that this behaviour was criminal; others were told that there was no legal duty to rescue. The former group judged the inaction more harshly than the latter group. Breaking the law was in itself viewed as immoral. Similarly, Walker and Marsh (1984) discovered that subjects stated that their disapproval of not wearing a seat-belt would increase when this became an offence.

While the mere existence of criminal laws has important expressive consequences, it is enforcement of that law and the punishment of offenders that gives the criminal law its real 'sting'. Through punishment society is emphatically condemning and thereby disavowing the offender's acts. Failure to punish, on the other hand, amounts to an endorsement or approval of such actions. Feinberg (1965) uses a telling example: suppose an aeroplane from nation A shoots down an aeroplane from nation B over international waters. If nation A were to punish its pilot this would amount to a disavowal of the pilot's action: the actions would simply be those of a deranged pilot. But a failure to punish the pilot would amount to an endorsement of his actions. Nation A would effectively be admitting that it was responsible for the act and approved of it.

Such disavowals of criminal acts have an important socialising effect in reinforcing attitudes and social values. They are part of the conditioning process that creates conscious and unconscious inhibitions against committing crime. In this way the criminal law can have the effect of strengthening the public's moral code. Every time a person is punished for, say, theft, our underlying conviction that theft is wrong is reinforced. The aim of punishing drunken drivers is not simply to deter other would-be drunken drivers but to try and induce a social climate in which it is regarded as morally unacceptable to drive after drinking too much alcohol.

Acceptance of these views has important implications for the structuring of substantive criminal offences. If the function of the criminal law and punishment is largely an expressive, symbolic one, it is important that the messages to be communicated be informative. For instance, single broad offences would be morally confusing. The law must state clearly, for example, that both murder and manslaughter are unacceptable wrongs, but it must point out the *level of rejection* of each activity by different punishment levels. Bearing this expressive function more clearly in mind would also lead to a clearer relationship between different offences, for example, theft, handling stolen goods and fraud. The enquiry would simply be: how crucial are the values embodied in each of these offences, *relative to each other*? The answer to this question would reveal how necessary it was to disavow deviation from those values; appropriate levels of punishment would emerge.

A lesser, but related, claim is that even if criminal law and punishment does not actually mould morality, it nevertheless induces an automatic, habitual response of obeying the law. A soldier in the army might not believe in the justice or morality of every order he receives, but he has been indoctrinated into a knee-jerk habit of obeying all orders. The criminal law and punishment can induce such law-abiding conduct 'purely as a matter of habit, with fear, respect for authority or social imitation as connecting links' (Andenaes, 1952).

Punishment for the purpose of inducing the habit of conformity to the law might be necessary for other psychological reasons. Durkheim (1964) has argued that those who obey the law need support. At a subconscious level there might be a temptation to commit crime. By abstaining therefrom, the conformist has been able to maintain internal control. To sustain this balance within the personality and ensure the dominance of internal control, the conformist needs to be able to identify with the police and the courts; the offender must be made unattractive as a role model. The inhibition of deviant impulses must be made to seem worthwhile. The punishment of offenders reassures the conformist that it was worth obeying the law. His morale and habit of not breaking the law are maintained.

2. Deterrence

A more traditional explanation of the function of the criminal law is that the threat of punishment for violating that law operates as a deterrent. Unlike the above idea of utilising the criminal law to reaffirm social values (often called 'educative deterrence'), the threat of punishment operates here at a conscious level, inducing people to refrain from crime. Deterrent punishment can operate in one of two ways.

With *individual deterrence* the hope is that the offender being punished will find the experience so unpleasant that he will not reoffend. It is extremely difficult to test the efficacy of this. Statistics as to the number of offenders not reconvicted (and who might therefore have been deterred as a result of their previous punishment) are of limited utility unless one knows *why* they did not reoffend (and what percentage did commit further crimes but were not apprehended).

With *general deterrence* the punishment of the offender is aimed at the public at large in the hope that the example and threat of punishment will deter them from crime. This operates in two ways. First, regular and normal levels of punishment keep the constant threat of similar punishment alive. Secondly, courts will occasionally pass 'exemplary sentences'. These are disproportionately severe penalties usually imposed when a particular type of activity is on the increase. For instance, concern over the rise of football hooliganism led to the exemplary sentence of life imprisonment for riotous assembly outside a football ground in *Whitton* (1985) – (a sentence reduced to three years' imprisonment on appeal [*Whitton*, 1986]: see page 196).

The theory of general deterrence rests entirely upon one assumption – that people are in fact deterred from committing crime by the threat of punishment. It is crucial therefore that the public know about punishments being imposed. Such publicity is most easily obtained when exemplary sentences are imposed (but is probably counterbalanced by the extensive coverage given to the occasional 'lenient' sentence – as when a rapist is fined). News media coverage of 'normal' punishments is far more selective and mainly confined to local papers – and even there it is the circumstances of the offence and the identity of the offender that attract most attention (Walker, 1985).

There are several celebrated examples purporting to demonstrate the effectiveness of deterrent sentencing. For instance, in 1919 the police went on strike in Liverpool. With the chances of apprehension significantly reduced, the crime rate (especially looting of shops) escalated sharply. Similar results occurred when the Nazis occupied Denmark in 1944 and arrested the entire police force – the general crime rate rose sharply and immediately.

Much of the current research on deterrence has been based on an economic model. The potential criminal is seen as a rational calculator who balances the costs and benefits of his possible actions. The 'costs' include the probability of apprehension, the severity of punishment, the ease with which the crime can be committed, chances of success etc., while 'benefits' refers to the satisfaction, whether monetary or otherwise, to be derived from the crime. Feeding in other variables such as income, earning potential, environment, taste, employment status and education level, the thesis is that a person will only commit a crime if, according to his evaluation, the benefits will outweigh the costs (i.e. there is a net *utility* to be derived), and if this perceived utility exceeds that he could derive from alternative, lawful activities.

Becker (1968), in a pioneering article, hypothesised that an offence, O, could be expressed as the function

$$O = O\,(p, f, u)$$

where p is the probability of conviction, f is the expected punishment and u is a composite variable representing all the other influences. In order for deterrence to be effective and crime to be reduced, the costs must be made to outweigh the benefits. Increasing the probability of conviction or the severity of the punishment would make the prospect of crime less attractive and induce the individual not to commit crimes. As p, f and u are all functions of O, albeit without precise values, it follows that crimes with low detection rates would need correspondingly higher penalties. The importance of the other variables must not be forgotten. For instance, if education could be increased and unemployment reduced, the utility to be gained from lawful employment might outweigh that to be derived from crime.

Several empirical studies based on this economic model of crime have been carried out and indicate some support for the thesis. For instance, Ehrlich (1973) found that a 1 per cent increase in p (probability of conviction) was associated with a crime reduction of 0.99 per cent, and a 1 per cent increase in f (expected punishment) was associated with a crime reduction of 1.12 per cent.

Such an economic analysis of criminal motivation and the entire theory of general deterrence is based upon an assumption that people are always rational and think before they act. They are 'rational utility maximisers', which means that prospective gains and losses are weighed against each other with decisions and choices being based on such a calculus. While this might be true of some individuals and some crimes (for instance, one might rationally calculate the gains and losses in parking on a double yellow line), it is clearly not true of all individuals and crimes. Many crimes (particularly those involving violence) are often committed by persons in highly emotional states who are acting in an exceedingly irrational manner. The man who, in a fury, beats his wife to death is hardly a 'rational utility maximiser'; his motivation is anger, jealousy, love, hate or whatever and he is simply not amenable to deterrence at that point. Similarly, many other persons are not deterrable: the mentally disordered, the intoxicated, the addict etc. The criminal law might have *some* effect with some of such persons in inducing some care in the commission of the crime – for instance, a drug addict might not purchase drugs right in front of a policeman – but it will never deter him from committing the crime altogether.

Deterrence can only be effective if people think that there is a reasonable prospect that they will be caught. A man wishing to bugger his consenting wife is hardly going to be deterred by the maximum penalty of life imprisonment for his offence (assuming he was a criminal lawyer and aware of the ludicrous penalty!). He knows that he will not be apprehended and so will not be deterred. So what are the criminal's actual chances of being caught? The Criminal Statistics (1984) reveal that only 35 per cent of notifiable offences were cleared up by the police. Countless offences, however, are never reported to the police and so, of course, never cleared up. For instance, it has been estimated that only 8 per cent of robberies and thefts from the person are recorded by the police (the estimates vary significantly from crime to crime: for example, 48 per cent for burglary in a dwelling and 98 per cent for theft of a motor vehicle). And it must be borne in mind that 'cleared up' does not mean convicted – but covers all cases where there is sufficient evidence to charge a person. The overall picture is thus a clear one: crime pays; the criminal's chances of not being caught are far higher than those of being apprehended. Further, if one examines the clear-up rate per offence (again, of those recorded by the police) one discovers that generally the offences for which one is most likely to be apprehended (homicide – 91 per cent; assault – 89 per cent) are those that are often committed impulsively or by persons not amenable to deterrence while the clear-up rate for crimes more likely to be committed 'rationally' is even lower than the general average (burglary in a dwelling – 25 per cent).

Of course, in assessing the efficacy of deterrent punishment, the actual statistics on clear-up rates are not helpful unless the prospective criminal is aware of them. What matters is the individual's assessment of his prospects of apprehension. If he thinks there is a 95 per cent chance of being caught if he burgles a house, then he will probably be deterred and it is irrelevant that his assessment of the risk is hopelessly awry. There are no reliable statistics on this. Willcock and Stokes (1968) discovered that the young persons they surveyed tended to overrate their chances of detection. However, while many persons might be overcautious in their estimate of the risks, it would not be unreasonable to assume that many others will think they are 'too smart' to get caught – and once they start committing crimes they will become part of the statistical pattern; their assessment of the risks will become more accurate and, knowing the truth, they will be less likely to be deterred.

Apart from the anecdotal, it is difficult to obtain clear evidence as to the deterrent effect of sentencing (Beyleveld 1980). Judges, perhaps in desperation, continue to have faith in the deterrent impact of their sentences. Perhaps the most realistic view is that expressed by one of the leading penologists in Britain, Walker (1985), who concludes that '*some* people can be deterred in *some* situations from *some* types of conduct by *some* degree of likelihood that they will be penalised in *some* ways.'

3. Incapacitation

Another commonly stated function of the criminal law is the protection of society by the incapacitation of dangerous offenders. Crime is reduced by restricting the offender's opportunity to commit further crimes.

Most societies allow for some special form of protective sentencing. In England an 'extended sentence' (a sentence in excess of that normally permissible for the offence) can be imposed upon an offender when his previous record and the likelihood of his committing further offences makes it 'expedient to protect the public from him for a substantial time' (Powers of the Criminal Courts Act 1973, section 28). Similarly, with the wide array of offences carrying a maximum penalty of life imprisonment (for example, rape, causing grievous bodily harm with intent, aggravated burglary etc.) the sentencing judge can impose such a maximum penalty upon an offender perceived to be dangerous to society. Finally, it must be remembered that non-custodial protective sentences can be imposed. Thus disqualifying an offender from driving is regarded as one of the most effective means of protecting road-users from dangerous drivers. Fortunately, other more barbaric forms of incapacitative sentence, such as the cutting off of limbs, deportation to Australia and capital punishment, are no longer with us today.

Two widely differing examples of protective sentencing will help reveal the nature of, and the difficulties with, utilising the criminal law and the process of punishment for this purpose. In *Nicholls* (1970) the offender was convicted of one count of indecent assault on a girl aged seven. He had no less than nine previous convictions for indecent assault and attempted rape of children aged between four and nine years of age. The court imposed an extended sentence of ten years' imprisonment on the basis that the offender was a danger to the public. The other case is a famous and controversial United States Supreme Court decision, *Rummel v. Estelle* (1980) in which a sentence of life imprisonment for obtaining $120.75 by false pretences was affirmed. The defendant had two previous convictions: fraudulent use of a credit card to obtain $80 worth of goods (nine years previously), and passing a forged cheque of $28.36 (four years previously). He was prosecuted under a Texas recidivist statute making life imprisonment mandatory upon a third felony conviction. A majority in the Supreme Court rejected a claim that life imprisonment was a grossly disproportionate punishment and held that it was legitimate for a state to segregate recidivists from the rest of society 'for an extended period of time'.

The contrast between these two cases leads us directly to a consideration of two central problems associated with sentencing on such bases. First, how is 'dangerousness' to be defined for these purposes? Most people would agree that Nicholls with his persistent sexual aggression constituted a 'danger' to children. But can the same be said of Rummel? If protective sentencing is to be employed, it must surely be limited to those who are dangerous in the sense of being likely to cause *serious harms*. Of course, this approach in itself raises problems. While most would agree that death, serious bodily injury and serious sexual assault clearly qualify as serious harms for this purpose, controversy arises in relation to a host of other harms, for example, 'loss or damage to property which results in severe personal hardship' (Floud Committee, 1981). One thing does, however, seem certain. It could not be seriously asserted that the kind of offence Rummel might in future commit could possibly justify the imposition of a sentence of life imprisonment.

The second problem is one of predicting or identifying dangerousness. How probable must it be that Nicholls or Rummel will offend again before we are justified in imposing an incapacitative sentence? How immediate, how frequent and how specific must the risk be? Numerous research projects have recently been undertaken aimed at developing accurate criteria for predicting dangerousness. For instance, Greenwood (1982) developed a seven-factor prediction index (based on previous criminal history, drug use and unemployment) to identify persons likely to commit frequent acts of robbery or other violent crimes in future. The problem with this and many other projects is that research has been based on the admissions of *imprisoned offenders* only, which has prompted the cynical response that this is 'like trying to learn about the smoking habits of smokers generally by studying the smoking activity of residents of a lung cancer ward' (von Hirsch, 1986). Even more serious is the fact that such projects to date have tended to yield rather too many 'false positives' (classifications of dangerousness that did not materialise).

This last point is critical. A 'false positive' is not just a statistic. It is a human being locked up in prison because society has made a mistake in wrongly predicting him to be dangerous. Accordingly, until such time as more accurate prediction criteria have been developed (if this is ever possible) it must be highly questionable whether punishment for such reasons can be justified. The related question of whether it can *ever* be permissible to punish people on the basis of what they might do in the future will be considered in the final section of this book.

4. Rehabilitation

Few would dissent from the proposition that it would be in everyone's interests if offenders could be rehabilitated. If most offenders became reformed individuals who were less inclined to commit further crimes, a huge step towards the overall objective of crime reduction would have been achieved. But while there is general agreement that rehabilitation is a desirable *by-product* of punishment, controversy arises when it is asserted that rehabilitation is one of the *main purposes* of the institution of punishment.

Over the past century our criminal justice system has become more concerned with the rehabilitation and welfare of convicted offenders. Many reforms to the prison system have been instituted, with increasing emphasis being placed on training and educational programmes within prisons so that employment prospects on release will be enhanced. More significant, however, has been the recognition that imprisonment necessarily involves the isolation of the offender from the realities of social life which can hardly be conducive to the rehabilitative process. Prisoners tend to become institutionalised and dependent on a system that relieves them of the responsibility of having to control their own destiny. If, on the other hand, offenders could be kept in society and forced (with help) to deal with the real world while being encouraged to understand and assume responsibility, rehabilitation could be more easily achieved. To reflect this latter philosophy various non-custodial sentences have been introduced into English law, particularly probation and community service orders.

With rehabilitative sentencing emphasis is placed on the offender; he is regarded as 'sick' and in need of a cure. Like a doctor prescribing medicine, the sentencer must impose that sentence predicted to be most effective in making the offender better. This leads to 'individualisation' of sentencing. Punishment is made to fit the offender and not the crime. With less emphasis being placed on the crime committed, the result is that two offenders committing similar crimes can receive very different sentences if their 'needs' are not the same.

While such ideas have a certain humanitarian appeal, the fact remains that it is almost impossible to justify rehabilitation as a *purpose* of punishment. There are several reasons for this. First, we know very little of the causes of crime and so have limited knowledge of how to change people's behaviour and eliminate their propensity to commit crime. The result is that efforts to tailor the sentence to fit the offender are almost inevitably doomed to failure: Martinson (1974) concluded that rehabilitative sentencing simply did not work; the type of sentence given to an offender made no difference to the likelihood of his being reconvicted. While this is now widely recognised as a gross exaggeration (even Martinson, 1976, partially retracted his earlier sweeping conclusions), the fact remains that it is extremely difficult to assess accurately the rehabilitative effect of any given sentence and the research to date has been inconclusive as to the efficacy of such sentencing. However, one thing seems certain: the overall picture painted by penologists is so pessimistic that one could never be justified in claiming that it was legitimate to sentence offenders primarily for the purpose of reforming them.

Rehabilitative sentencing can also be attacked on other grounds. Eliminating a person's propensity to commit crime involves altering his personality so that he no longer wants to commit crime. Is one entitled to use any means to achieve this result – even drugs, aversion and electric shock therapy or psychosurgery? And for how long is one entitled to continue such 'treatment'? These questions raise the fundamental human rights issues of whether we have the moral right to change a person's personality without his consent. The commission of a crime does not deprive one of all basic human rights so that one can be treated as an experimental guinea-pig. As Morris and Hawkins (1977) have asserted: 'We must stay out of the business of forcibly remaking man.'

The final nail in the coffin of the rehabilitative ideal occurred when research began to reveal the extent to which rehabilitation was leading to sentencing disparity. People committing broadly similar crimes were receiving vastly different sentences – under the guise of individualised sentencing. In the United States, particularly, concern over the extent of such sentencing disparity, coupled with the publication of research indicating that rehabilitative sentencing was not effective, led to the swift and sudden demise of the rehabilitative ideal and its replacement by the notion that one must sentence people according to what they deserve (see later, page 193).

For all these reasons it seems clear that one is not justified in punishing in order to accomplish rehabilitative objectives. But that is not to say that rehabilitation is of no consequence. Indeed, one of the dangers of minimising its importance is that it could induce those managing the criminal justice system, particularly those involved in executing sentences such as prison warders, to become more punitive minded, or even vindictive, in their approach to their work. A civilised and humane society cannot afford to ignore the importance of rehabilitating offenders. What this means is that while one might be punishing for other reasons such as deterrence or incapacitation, rehabilitation must remain a desirable *collateral objective*. When espoused as a *purpose* of punishment, rehabilitation becomes vulnerable and in danger of being jettisoned if found to be ineffective. But if clearly understood as a desirable by-product or collateral purpose, the rehabilitative ideal becomes immune from attack on grounds of inefficacy. Put crudely: it doesn't matter if we are successful in reforming people because that is not the object of the exercise – but in trying to achieve our main objectives we should at least try to rehabilitate offenders (subject to any human rights constraints). This is the humane course of action and any success would be of immense additional advantage.

D. ENFORCEMENT OF THE CRIMINAL LAW

We saw earlier that the mere existence of a particular law can have some symbolic impact (page 177). But, for the most part, if the criminal law hopes to be effective in achieving its objectives there must be a certain degree of actual enforcement of the law. The task of defining this necessary degree or level of enforcement, however, raises controversial political issues. These will be sketched briefly in this section.

The costs of crime are incalculable but generally agreed to be enormous. For instance, it has been estimated that fraud in the UK financial community results in losses of £750 million a year (Levi, 1986). Non-economic costs must also be considered: for instance, fear of violence on the streets in urban areas can cause intense anxiety and restrict the social activities of persons, diminishing the quality of their lives (Maxfield, 1984). However, on the other side of the balance sheet the costs of enforcing the criminal law are similarly astronomic. It costs in excess of £3000 million to maintain the police force (Cmnd 8789, 1983). Additionally there are the costs of the criminal courts, legal personnel, prisons, the probation service and so on. And yet, despite this investment, most crimes are never even reported to the police and, of those that are, only a minority are 'cleared up' (see page 182).

Clearly full enforcement of the criminal law is out of the question. The economic costs would be unthinkable and so also would be the social costs of living in a police state with a concomitant erosion of civil liberties and individual rights. The problem of shaping penal policy thus becomes the political one of determining the extent to which resources should be allocated to enforcement of the criminal law (as compared to the entire economy). The answer to this is necessarily shaped by other political considerations. For instance, those who see a clear link between crime and unemployment, inner-city decay and deprivation will obviously favour greater investment in tackling these social problems which will necessarily involve less direct expenditure on criminal law enforcement. Yet this is not the only resource allocation decision that needs to be made. Of the criminal justice allocation, how much should be spent on the police, how much on the courts, on prisons etc.? And within each component – say, the police – how much should be devoted to each of the numerous branches or departments thereof?

During the 1960s in Britain a certain degree of consensus existed on many fronts. There was a belief in the rehabilitative ideal and in the welfare state: greater expenditure in the latter would tackle the underlying causes of crime and thereby reduce the incidence of crime.

The 1970s, however, saw a sharp polarisation of political opinion with the emergence of a 'law and order' lobby who, impatient with perceived 'softness' towards criminals, began demanding increased police powers and tougher sentences for criminals. The Conservative Party embraced many of these ideas and won the 1979 election with an election manifesto placing 'law and order' high on its lists of priorities. The adoption of such a platform is hardly surprising given the Conservative Government's overall policy of returning to 'traditional values' which include a great emphasis on discipline and individual responsibility and increasing scepticism of the welfare state. According to this view offenders cannot hide behind the 'excuse' of social deprivation but must bear full responsibility for their actions which necessarily means they must be *caught* and then *punished*.

In pursuing these objectives the Conservative Government passed the Criminal Justice Act 1982 (attempting to deal more firmly with young offenders in particular) and has increased sentences for certain crimes (attempted rape and trafficking in Class A drugs). Further 'law and order' statutes such as the Public Order Act 1986 and the Drug Trafficking Offences Act 1986 have recently been enacted. But most significant has been the government's endorsement of the status and powers of the police. Determined to strengthen the image and moral authority of the police who are at the 'cutting edge' of the criminal justice system, the government awarded substantial pay increases to them (greatly in excess of those awarded to other public servants) and enacted the Police and Criminal Evidence Act 1984 clarifying and strengthening police powers significantly. In terms of the punishment of offenders, the 'law and order' policy can be seen in the investment of large sums in new building programmes for prisons (Morgan, 1983).

However, despite this greater commitment to enforcement of the criminal law, no measurable reduction in crime has ensued. In fact, it would seem that the only hope (and it can be no more than that) of achieving such a reduction would involve such a vast increase in enforcement expenditure as to be both morally and economically unacceptable. Accordingly, it might be better to adopt more realistic goals in terms of crime reduction and to devote more attention to ensuring that the criminal law is applied in a fair and just manner. Over the last decade this has become a matter of utmost concern to those involved in the criminal law and its application – and it is to this final topic that we now turn.

E. JUSTICE AND DESERT

The function of the criminal law is to identify that conduct which ought to be criminalised and to try and reduce the incidence of such activity. However, there are severe restrictions on the way in which the law can attempt to achieve this objective.

First, in a civilised society cruel or barbaric punishment must be impermissible. Even if it could be scientifically proven that the incidence of theft would be reduced by cutting off the hands of thieves, such an option would simply be unacceptable. The same is true of corporal and capital punishment. A society resorting to controlled, explicit violence against its offenders reduces itself to their level. The hypocrisy of claiming that murder, for instance, is wrong while indulging in ritualised killing is manifest and robs the criminal law of its claim to moral authority. It simply becomes an assertion of power. There are views opposed to this but one hopes the role of such punishments in Britain can be assigned to the history books and so the argument here will not be pursued.

A second and more problematic issue relates to the distribution of punishment. Assuming one is not dealing with a cruel or inhumane form of punishment, whom is one permitted to punish and to what extent in order to seek a reduction of crime? For instance, could one impose a sentence of life imprisonment for minor theft? Could one punish the children of an offender if this were felt to be an effective deterrent? If we punished someone (anyone!) every time a burglary were committed, the level of such criminal activity would almost surely be reduced by knowledge of such a '100 per cent clear-up rate'. But would such sentences be justifiable?

In discharging its functions the criminal law must be structured and applied in a *just* and *fair* manner that is capable of commanding general respect. This means that the type of conduct made criminal, the structure and definitions of the criminal law and the extent of punishment must be accepted by the bulk of society. It is thus crucial that the criminal law reflects everyday values: the way we live our lives and treat each other. Integral to these values is the notion of *desert*. Think of the everyday responses: 'he deserved to pass his exams'; 'the way they played, they deserved to lose the cricket match'. What people deserve depends on the extent to which we praise or blame them for their actions and the results of their actions. We praise an actor's performance in the cinema and say, 'He deserves an Oscar'; we blame the football team that plays poorly and without spirit all season and say, 'They deserve to be relegated to the bottom division.'

We have seen throughout this book that generally the criminal law is structured so as to reflect these fundamental values. When a blameworthy actor causes a harm (in an area appropriately criminalised) punishment is *deserved*. We have similarly seen that there are degrees of blame and harm. Causing death is 'worse' than causing bodily harm. Intentionally causing death is 'worse' than recklessly causing it. It follows that the amount of punishment deserved varies with the degree of blame and harm. In other words the entire structure of the criminal law with related punishment levels depends on this notion of desert. It would make no sense to construct an entire system on the premise of desert and then, when it came to punishment, to jettison all such reasoning and resort to pure crime prevention tactics. It is thus clear in principle: no punishment can be imposed unless it is *deserved*. Life imprisonment for minor theft is not deserved; the children of an offender and other innocent persons do not deserve punishment so that others may be deterred.

Some writers have pushed this idea of desert further and have asserted that the *purpose* of the whole institution of punishment is to give offenders their just deserts. By committing a crime they have gained an unfair advantage over other members of society who have exercised restraint. They must be punished in order to eliminate that advantage and restore social equilibrium. This seems a rather metaphysical justification for the infliction of suffering upon others. There must surely be some greater purpose to the criminal law. It must be permissible at least to strive for some concrete benefit such as crime reduction. But in this quest it is crucial to recognise that the law must be subject to the *constraints of just desert* so that if one fails in one's objectives, at least it would not be a failure involving injustice (cynically called a 'failure model' of the criminal law by Rothman, 1981). Put another way, the function of the criminal law and punishment is to reduce crime – but one is only justified in punishing any given offender to the extent that he deserves punishment.

This way of thinking might seem uncontroversial when applied to the extreme examples earlier in this section. But that logic must be capable of general application. This means that the child-molesting defendant in *Nicholls* (1970) (see page 184), who received an extended sentence on the grounds of his dangerousness, was, to the extent that his sentence was extended, being punished more than he deserved. He was sentenced primarily on the basis of what he might do in the future. Similar reasoning can be applied to exemplary sentences, such as the one imposed on the football hooligan in *Whitton* (1985) (see page 180). He was being used as a means to some greater end, the deterrence of others – he did not deserve the penalty of life imprisonment initially imposed on him. Excessive rehabilitative sentencing can be similarly condemned. In *Greedy* (1964) a sentence was increased from three to five years' imprisonment 'to give time for treatment to be effective'. Assuming that three years was the 'deserved sentence', this defendant was sentenced to two years' undeserved imprisonment. In relation to this excess he was 'innocent' and, in principle, in the same position as our earlier more extreme hypothetical offenders.

While the concept of just desert is by no means new, it is only in the last decade that it has begun to assume a position of critical importance in criminal law thinking. Until then, belief in the possibility of crime reduction and enchantment with the rehabilitative ideal had held sway for much of this century. The 'just deserts' movement began in the 1970s in the United States and was primarily the result of two related factors. First, the demise of the rehabilitative ideal (see page 187) and second, mounting concern at the extent of sentencing disparity. The *injustice* of imposing hugely different sentences upon offenders convicted of similar crimes began to be stressed. Whether this was the result of 'individualisation' of sentencing or, more likely, judges simply being inconsistent and perhaps even idiosyncratic in their approach did not really matter. The result was the same. Justice demands equality of treatment. There is no justice when persons guilty of crimes of comparable seriousness receive vastly different punishments. The best way to eliminate such inequality is to limit judicial discretion in the sentencing decision, ensuring that the decision is the same irrespective of the judge.

A majority of states in the United States have attempted to give effect to such ideas by developing 'guideline models' of sentencing. The best known of these is the Minnesota Sentencing Guidelines Grid which operates as follows. All offences are ranked in a hierarchy of seriousness and are assigned an appropriate level of severity. Similarly, the offender is allocated a criminal history score by scoring points for each previous conviction (the value of these points varies depending on the seriousness of the prior convictions). The offence level and criminal history score are then arranged in the vertical and horizontal columns respectively of a grid. For every level of offence combined with a particular criminal history score there is a cell containing a presumptive penalty. *Slight* variation from this presumptive penalty is permitted within specified minima and maxima if mitigating or aggravating circumstances are found to exist. For instance, if a defendant with a criminal history score of 3 points commits aggravated robbery in Minnesota he will normally be sentenced to forty-nine months' imprisonment. The judge retains limited discretion in that this sentence can be varied if mitigating or aggravating circumstances are found to exist but the extent of such variation is severely restricted to a range of between forty-five and fifty-three months. Parole is abolished, thus eliminating discretion at the stage of release from prison ('good time' reductions still exist but can be accurately computed in advance). Under such a scheme comparable offenders (in the sense of their criminal record) committing the same crime will receive similar sentences.

There are very real problems with such guideline models of sentencing. First, most offences are defined in fairly broad bands, each encompassing a wide range of factual and moral distinctions.

For instance, two defendants with identical criminal records might both commit the (English) crime of robbery. The first defendant, motivated by a desperate family financial situation, threatens his victim with a walking stick and makes off with £10. The second defendant holds up a security van with a sawn-off shotgun and steals £100,000. It seems nonsense to assert that these two should obtain the same or very similar sentences. While this problem is less acute in the United States as offences are generally more closely defined than in Britain (for example, degrees of robbery exist in many states), it has nevertheless been recognized that the guideline method of sentencing ought to involve a more precise breakdown and subcategorisation of offences. We have seen at various stages of this book that there might be real advantages in such an approach – but if judicial discretion is to be virtually eliminated, each category of offence would need to be fairly closely defined, which could involve 'hammering out a definition of robbery in the 68th degree' (Executive Advisory Committee on Sentencing in New York, 1979). Such an exercise would not only be impracticable but also totally confusing in terms of the law's moral and educative role.

A second objection to these United States developments is that while they might succeed in controlling judicial discretion, they ignore the fact that the criminal justice system is riddled with discretion at every stage. Why attack *judicial* discretion when police and prosecutors have enormous discretionary powers as to whether to arrest and as to the actual offence charged. Indeed, abolishing judicial discretion could simply result in an increased shift of discretionary power to other officials, notably the prosecutor. Principles of equality of treatment and notions of receiving one's just deserts not only come into operation in the courtroom but have to be applied throughout the whole system.

Finally, such a sentencing model has clear dangers. The idea of mandatory minimum sentences which a guideline model effectively endorses (along with mandatory maxima) has long appealed to the law and order brigade as their response to a perceived ever-increasing crime rate. Such a sentencing model could then be used as a means of imposing stiffer prison sentences on more persons, resulting in a huge increase in the prison population. It ought to be stressed at this stage that the revived just deserts movement in the United States was not the brain-child of law and order thinking. It was first articulated by liberal thinkers concerned with injustice in the system and equally concerned to *lower* prison sentences. For instance, the Minnesota Sentencing Guideline Commission in developing its guidelines deliberately and overtly adopted a policy of prison population constraint (Minnesota Guidelines Report, 1980). One of the most influential early reports advocating the just deserts approach was the von Hirsch Committee (1976) which proposed that the highest penalty for any offence (save murder) should be five years' imprisonment – with sparing use made of sentences of imprisonment in excess of three years. However, the real reason behind the phenomenal success of the just deserts movement in the United States was the fact that this intellectually respectable theoretical framework provided by the liberals was politically convenient to the conservative law and order camp which was concerned at 'undue leniency'. The lesson is clear. The success of any guideline model of sentencing depends on the political composition of those drafting the guidelines and fixing the levels of sentence.

In England there has also been growing concern at the extent of sentencing disparity. Neither informed commentators nor the general public are any longer prepared to sweep such disparity under the carpet of 'individualised sentencing'. Whether it be a sudden outrageous sentence such as life imprisonment for a football hooligan (*Whitton*, 1985) or probation for a rapist, there is an increasing tendency for such cases to make front-page news and arouse concern. This is supported by a growing body of research clearly demonstrating that great sentencing disparity exists among the 27,000 magistrates handling 98 per cent of all criminal cases (Moxon, 1985). While one can appeal against sentences from the Magistrates' Court and from the Crown Court, thus eliminating gross discrepancies in sentencing (for example, the defendant in *Whitton*, 1985, had his sentence reduced from life imprisonment to three years' imprisonment), the fact remains that appeals from Magistrates' Courts are not common and appeals from the Crown Court require the leave of the Court of Appeal (Criminal Division). Further, the prosecution has no right of appeal – and it must be remembered that a disparate sentence can be an unduly lenient one as well as an unduly stiff one.

Accordingly the Court of Appeal (Criminal Division) in England has started issuing 'guideline judgments' in which judicial sentencing guidelines are laid down for particular offences, the idea being that a 'common law of sentencing' will emerge. These judgments consider a wide variety of circumstances in laying down appropriate levels of sentence. Let us consider one such case as an example. In *Billam* (1986) new sentencing guidelines were laid down for rape:

(a) where there are no aggravating or mitigating features five years' imprisonment should be the 'starting point' in contested cases;

(b) where the rape is committed by two or more men acting together or by a man who has broken into his victim's living accommodation (or in other stated instances) the 'starting point' should be eight years;

(c) where the rapist has committed the crime against a number of different women a sentence of fifteen years or more may be appropriate;

(d) where the defendant has manifested perverted or psychopathic tendencies indicating that he is dangerous to women, a life sentence will not be inappropriate.

The judgment then goes on to list aggravating and mitigating circumstances.

The obvious advantage of such judicial guidelines is their flexibility in comparison with legislatively endorsed guidelines as in the United States. But from another perspective this is also their weakness. As can be seen from the above example, the guidelines are broad and generalised and allow for a great deal of discretion by the sentencing judge. Further, they are designed 'for assistance only and are not to be used as rules never to be departed from' (*Nicholas*, 1986). Indeed, the existence of sentencing guidelines for football hooligans (*Wood*, 1984 – admittedly even more limited and generalised than usual) did not prevent the initial sentence of life imprisonment being imposed on the defendant in *Whitton* (1985).

In order to meet some of these objections, thereby giving the judicial guidelines more 'teeth', the present Conservative Government has proposed giving statutory force to the Court of Appeal's sentencing guidelines (Plans for Legislation, 1986).

Perhaps the best way forward is to construct a guideline model of sentencing that combines the best features of both the above systems and reflects a realistic philosophy of the criminal law and punishment. The problem with the models developed in the United States is that they are *too* committed to an exclusive endorsement of the just deserts doctrine. The result is inflexibility. While the role of just deserts is critical in the criminal law and its construction, that does not mean that it is the only consideration. One can never be justified in punishing a person more than he deserves. Rights to freedom can only be forfeited to an extent that is deserved. But the fact that one is justified in punishing a person does not mean that one *must* actually impose that punishment. For instance, my student might *deserve* to be reported to the police and prosecuted for stealing a library book but I might recognise that the humiliation of being caught and exposed to others in our institution will have a sufficient deterrent effect on him and others. Nothing would be achieved by reporting the matter to the police. I can afford mercy. There ought to be a good reason for inflicting suffering on other human beings and such reasons are best found in the utilitarian soil of deterrence, incapacitation and rehabilitation. Put simply, a man may have committed a certain crime meaning that he deserves three years' imprisonment. We therefore cannot sentence him to more than three years' imprisonment because we adjudge him to be dangerous or because we feel that an exemplary sentence might be effective in clamping down on the particular criminal activity. Three years is the maximum possible punishment. But that does not mean that he *must* receive the full deserved sentence. Whether we impose the maximum or something less depends on what we hope to achieve thereby. If he has been adjudged not to be dangerous or in need of rehabilitation and a punishment was being imposed primarily to uphold moral standards in society (educative deterrence), we might be able to impose a sentence of less than three years' imprisonment.

However, the demands of justice and equal treatment must be borne firmly in mind. It is important that if another student of mine is caught stealing a library book he be treated the same as the first. It would simply not be just to make a sacrificial lamb out of the second student having treated the first so differently. However, there must be room for some flexibility here – but that flexibility must be controlled. All the circumstances affecting a crime cannot be anticipated in advance and spelt out in a list of aggravating or mitigating circumstances. Accordingly there must be scope for some judicial discretion. But clear guidance needs to be provided as to the type and level of sentence that is appropriate in a given situation. Present offences are too broad, and judicial guidelines too generalised, for adequate control of judicial discretion.

What is needed is a guideline model for each offence or related groups of offence – say, one for theft and deception offences and another for offences against the person and so on. How thereafter to control judicial discretion while admitting some flexibility is the central problem. There are various possible compromise models that could be adopted here. For instance, one could have a *legislatively* fixed *maximum* sentence within each cell of the grid, with judicial guidelines indicating what the appropriate level of actual punishment in the circumstances should be. Alternatively, one could have a legislatively fixed *presumptive* penalty or range within each cell. Under either scheme any departure from the judicial guidelines or the presumptive penalty or range would need to be expressly justified by the sentencing judge and there would have to be a right of appeal in such cases.

Certain key issues would need resolving whichever model were adopted. Which aggravating and mitigating circumstances should be built into the substantive definitions of criminal offences? Which should be incorporated into the offence level of the grid? And which should be left to the sentencing judge to influence his decision whether to depart from the penalty within the grid? Should previous convictions be the only factors to be incorporated into the offender score – and if so, what weight should be attributed to such factors? This last question can only be answered by determining *why* previous convictions are relevant in the first place. Is it because an offender with previous convictions deserves more punishment because of his failure to learn from the experience of past punishment? Or is it because the guideline model represents a compromise between the just deserts philosophy and the desire to incapacitate perceived dangerous offenders?

These are difficult questions. Answers have not yet clearly emerged but it is in this field that the debate in criminal law will be waged. The days of the old-fashioned 'substantive criminal lawyer' who regarded punishment and sentencing as matters purely for penologists and philosophers are gone. The substantive rules of the criminal law and the punishment of offenders are too closely related for any step to be taken on one without considering the implications for the other. Whichever solution to the current sentencing debate ultimately prevails in Britain, it will have a profound effect on the structure and substance of the rules of the criminal law.

Bibliography

Andenaes, J. (1952), 'General Prevention', 43 *Journal of Criminal Law*, C & PS 176

Beale, Joseph H. Jr (1903), 'Retreat from a Murderous Assault', 16 *Harvard Law Review* 567

Becker, Gary (1968), 'Crime and Punishment: an Economic Approach', 76 *Journal of Political Economy*

Bentham, Jeremy (1789), *An Introduction to the Principles of Morals and Legislation*

Beyleveld, D (1980), *A Bibliography on General Deterrence Research*, London: Saxon House

Brett, P. (1963), *An Inquiry into Criminal Guilt*, London: Sweet and Maxwell

Butler Committee (1975), *Report of the Committee on Mentally Abnormal Offenders*, Cmnd 6244

Carlen, P. (1980), 'Radical Criminology, Penal Politics and the Rule of Law' in P. Carlen and M. Collison, eds. *Radical Issues in Criminology*, New Jersey: Barnes and Noble

Clarkson, C. M. V. and Keating, H. M. (1984), *Criminal Law: Text and Materials*, London: Sweet and Maxwell

Cmnd 8789 (1983) The Government's Expenditure Plans, 1983–84 to 1985–86

Columbia Law Review (1952) Note, 'The Failure to Rescue: A Comparative Study', 52 *Columbia Review* 631.

Criminal Law Revision Committee (1980), 14th Report, *Offences against the Person*, Cmnd 7844

Criminal Law Revision Committee (1984), 15th Report, *Sexual Offences*, Cmnd 9213

Criminal Statistics (1984), England and Wales, Cmnd 9621

Devlin, Lord (1959), 'Morals and the Criminal Law', 45 *Proceedings of the British Academy* 136, reprinted in *The Enforcement of Morals* (1965)

Diamond, A.S. (1950) *Primitive Law*, 2nd ed., London: Longman

Duff, R. A. (1980), 'Recklessness', *Criminal Law Review* 282

Dumuth, C. (1978), *'Sus'* : *a Report on the Vagrancy Act 1824*, London: Runnymede Trust

Durkheim, E. (1964), *The Division of Labour in Society*, New York: Free Press

Erlich, I. (1973), 'Participation in Illegitimate Activities: a Theoretical and Empirical Investigation' 81 *Journal of Political Economy*

Executive Advisory Committee on Sentencing in New York (1979), *Crime and Punishment in New York: An Inquiry into Sentencing and the Criminal Justice Systems*, Report to Governor Hugh L. Carey

Feinberg, Joel (1965), 'The Expressive Function of Punishment', *The Monist*, vol. 49, no. 3

Feinberg, Joel (1984), *Harm to Others (The Moral Limits of the Criminal Law*, vol. 1), New York: Oxford University Press

Feinberg, Joel (1985), *Offense to Others (The Moral Limits of the Criminal Law*, vol. 2), New York: Oxford University Press

Fletcher, George P. (1978), *Rethinking Criminal Law*, Boston: Little, Brown

Floud Committee (1981), *Dangerousness and Criminal Justice*, London: Heinemann

Gordon, Gerald H. (1978), *Criminal Law*, 2nd ed., Edinburgh: W. Green

Greenwood, Peter W. (1982), *Selective Incapacitation*, Santa Monica, Ca., Rand Corporation

Gross, Hyman (1979), *A Theory of Criminal Justice*, New York: Oxford University Press

Hart, H. L. A. (1968), *Punishment and Responsibility*, Oxford University Press

Hart, H. L. A. and Honoré, A. M. (1985), *Causation in the Law*, 2nd ed., Oxford University Press

Holmes, O. W. (1881) *The Common Law*

James Committee (1975), *Report of the Committee on the Distribution of Criminal Business between the Crown Court and Magistrates' Courts*, Cmnd 6323

Justice (1980), *Breaking the Rules*, London: JUSTICE

Kadish, S. (1967), 'The Crisis of Overcriminalisation', 374 *Annals* 157.

Kadish, S. (1976), 'Respect for Life and Regard for Rights in the Criminal Law', 64 *California Law Review* 871

Kaufmann, (1970) 'Legality and Harmfulness of a Bystander's Failure to Intervene as Determinants of Moral Judgement' in J. Macaulay and L. Berkowitz, eds., *Altruism and Helping Behaviour: Social Psychological Studies of Some Antecedants and Consequences*, London: Academic Press

LaFave, W. R. and Scott A. W. (1972), *Criminal Law*, New York, West Publishing Co.

Lanham, D. (1976), 'Larsonneur Revisited', *Criminal Law Review* 276

Bibliography

Law Commission (1973) Law Commission Working Paper No. 50, *Inchoate Offences: Conspiracy, Attempt and Incitement*

Law Commission (1980) Law Commission Working Paper No. 102, *Attempt, and Impossibility in Relation to Attempt, Conspiracy and Incitment*

Law Commission (1985) Law Commission Working Paper No. 143, *Codification of the Criminal Law*

Leigh, L. H. (1982), *Strict and Vicarious Liability*, London: Sweet and Maxwell

Levi, M. (1986), unpublished Home Office research study, reported in the *Observer*, 9 February

Maguire, M. (1980), 'The Impact of Burglary upon Victims', *British Journal of Criminology* 261

Martinson, R. (1974), 'What Works? Questions and Answers about Prison Reform', 22 *Public Interest*, Spring

Martinson, R. (1976), *Rehabilitation, Recidivism and Research*, London: National Council on Crime and Delinquency

Maxfield M. (1984), 'Fear of Crime in England and Wales', Home Office Research Study No. 78

John Stuart Mill (1859), *On Liberty*

Minnesota Guidelines Report (1980), Minnesota Sentencing Guidelines Commission, *Report to the Legislature*, 2–3 (1 January)

Model Penal Code (1953) American Law Institute, Model Penal Code, Tentative Draft No. 1, Appendix A

Model Penal Code (1962) American Law Institute, Model Penal Code, Proposed Official Draft

Morgan, N. (1983), 'Non-custodial Penal Sanctions in England and Wales: a New Eutopia?' *Howard Journal*, vol. XXII, 148

Morris, N. (1951), 'Somnambulistic Homicide: Ghosts, Spiders and North Koreans', V *Res Judicatae*

Morris, N. and Hawkins, G. (1977) *Letter to the President on Crime Control*, University of Chicago Press

Morris, N. (1982), *Madness and the Criminal Law*, University of Chicago Press

Moxon, David, ed. (1985), *Managing Criminal Justice*, Home Office Research and Planning Unit

Nixon, Richard (1970), *New York Times*, 25 October, s. 1, p. 71

Plans for Legislation (1986), *Criminal Justice, Plans for Legislation*, Cmnd 9658

Posner, Richard A. (1985), 'An Economic Theory of the Criminal Law', 85 *Columbia Law Review* 1193

203

Queen's Bench Foundation (1976), *Rape – Prevention and Resistance*

Robinson, Paul (1982), 'Criminal Law Defences: a Systematic Analysis', 82 *Columbia Law Review* 199

Rothman, David (1981) 'Doing Time: Days, Months and Years in the Criminal Justice System' in H. Gross and A. von Hirsch, eds., *Sentencing*, New York: Oxford University Press

Royal Commission on Capital Punishment (1953), *Report of the Royal Commission on Capital Punishment*, Cmd 8932

Sayre, F. B. (1932), 'Mens Rea', 45 *Harvard Law Review* 974

Schulhofer, S. J. (1974), 'Harm and Punishment: a Critique of Emphasis on Results of Conduct in the Criminal Law', 122 *University of Pennsylvania Law Review*

Schulhofer, S. J. (1985), 'Is There an Economic Theory of Crime?', in *Nomos XXVII: Criminal Justice*, Part IV

Smith, J. C. (1981), Comment to *R. v. Caldwell, Criminal Law Review* 393

Smith, J.C. (1983), Comment to *R. v. Sullivan, Criminal Law Review* 257

Smith, J. C. (1985), Comment to *Kong Cheuk Kwan v. The Queen, Criminal Law Review* 788

Spencer, J. R. (1985), 'Handling, Theft and the Mala Fide Purchaser', *Criminal Law Review* 92

von Hirsch, A. (1986), 'Deservedness and Dangerousness in Sentencing Policy', *Criminal Law Review* 79

von Hirsch Committee (1976), *Doing Justice, The Choice of Punishments* (Report of the Committee for the Study of Incarceration)

Walker, N. and McCabe, S. (1968), *Crime and Insanity in England*, vol. 1, Edinburgh University Press

Walker N. (1985), *Sentencing Theory, Law and Practice*, London: Butterworth

Walker, N. and Marsh, C. (1984), 'Do Sentences Affect Public Disapproval?' 24 *British Journal of Criminology* 27

Wasik, M. (1979), 'Mens Rea, Motive and the Problem of "Dishonesty" in the Law of Theft', *Criminal Law Review* 543

West, D. J. (1965), *Murder Followed by Suicide*, London: Heinemann

Will, G. F. (1985), 'Let Us Now Praise Anger', *Newsweek*, 14 January

Willcock, H. D. and Stokes, J. (1968), *Deterrents to Crime among Youths of 15 to 21*, London: Government Social Survey Report, no. SS 356

Williams, Glanville (1978), *Textbook of Criminal Law*, 1st ed., London: Stevens and Sons

Williams, Glanville (1981), 'Recklessness Redefined', *Criminal Law Journal* 252

Bibliography

Williams, Glanville (1982), 'Divergent Interpretations of Recklessness', 132 *New Law Journal* 289, 313, 336

Williams, Glanville (1983), *Textbook of Criminal Law*, 2nd ed., London: Stevens and Sons

Wolfenden Committee (1957), *Report of the Committee on Homosexual Offences and Prostitution*, Cmd 247

Yale Law Journal (1980) Note, 'Property Theft Enforcement and the Criminal Secondary Purchaser of Stolen Goods', 89 *Yale Law Journal* 1225

Cases

Numbers in bold type refer to pages in the text

Cases

Cases

Cases

210

Cases

Statutes

Statutes

Statutes

FOREIGN STATUTES

Index

Index

Index

Index